Developing Projects Using Object-Oriented C++

Jo Ann Smith

COURSE TECHNOLOGY

ONE MAIN STREET, CAMBRIDGE, MA 02142

an International Thomson Publishing company I(T)P®

Cambridge • Albany • Bonn • Boston • Cincinnati • London • Madrid • Melbourne • Mexico City
New York • Paris • San Francisco • Singapore • Tokyo • Toronto • Washington

Developing Projects Using Object-Oriented C++ is published by Course Technology.

Managing Editor	Kristen Duerr
Product Manager	Cheryl Ouellette
Associate Product Manager	Margarita Donovan
Developmental Editor	Jessica Evans
Production Editor	Ellina Beletsky
Text Designer	Kim Munsell
Cover Designer	Efrats Reis

© 1999 by Course Technology— I**T**P®
A division of International Thomson Publishing

For more information contact:

Course Technology
One Main Street
Cambridge, MA 02142

International Thomson Editores
Seneca, 53
Colonia Polanco
11560 Mexico D.F. Mexico

ITP Europe
Berkshire House 168-173
High Holborn
London WCIV 7AA
England

ITP GmbH
Königswinterer Strasse 418
53227 Bonn
Germany

Nelson ITP Australia
102 Dodds Street
South Melbourne, 3205
Victoria, Australia

ITP Asia
60 Albert Street, #15-01
Albert Complex
Singapore 189969

ITP Nelson Canada
1120 Birchmount Road
Scarborough, Ontario
Canada M1K 5G4

ITP Japan
Hirakawacho Kyowa Building, 3F
2-2-1 Hirakawacho
Chiyoda-ku, Tokyo 102
Japan

Trademarks
Course Technology and the open book logo are registered trademarks and CourseKits is a trademark of Course Technology. Custom Editions is a registered trademark of International Thomson Publishing, Inc.

I**T**P® The ITP logo is a registered trademark of International Thomson Publishing.

Some of the product names and company names used in this book have been used for identification purposes only, and may be trademarks or registered trademarks of their respective manufacturers and sellers.

Disclaimer
Course Technology reserves the right to revise this publication and make changes from time to time in its content without notice.

ISBN 0-7600-1107-9

Printed in the United States of America

1 2 3 4 5 6 7 8 9 10 MZ 03 02 01 00 99

Preface

Developing Projects Using Object-Oriented C++ is designed to provide students with an opportunity to develop object-oriented C++ programs that they might encounter in a real-life programming environment. Throughout the book, students practice designing and developing C++ programs, as well as modifying and debugging existing C++ programs. Students also have an opportunity to develop large-scale applications and add functionality to them throughout the term. You can use this book to supplement any object-oriented C++ programming text. Although this book provides a review of C++ concepts, it assumes that students will learn concepts in more detail and depth from a textbook or from the instructor.

Organization and Coverage

Developing Projects Using Object-Oriented C++ contains seven chapters. Each chapter reviews important concepts that students will have learned in their C++ class. Each section of the chapter contains several exercises from three categories—Modify, Debug, and Develop—that reinforce the section's contents. Four larger-scale projects appear at the end of each chapter. Two of the projects continue throughout the book, allowing students to add functionality or modify the application during the term. Students will complete the two independent, smaller projects while they learn the concepts presented in that chapter.

When students finish with this book, they will have gained extensive practice in developing large- and small-scale programs and in modifying or debugging C++ programs written by another programmer.

Approach

Developing Projects Using Object-Oriented C++ distinguishes itself from other C++ books because of its unique approach, which provides students with the opportunity to solve problems that they might encounter as real-life programmers. Much of a programmer's time is spent maintaining existing code either by modifying or debugging programs. Many traditional textbooks include problems where students must develop their own programs from scratch. Students, however, also need practice in reading programs written by other programmers, understanding these programs, and then making modifications that might add functionality, change the methods employed to store data, or correct problems with the code. This book provides that practice.

Another distinguishing characteristic is the incremental approach to program development used in the end-of-chapter Progressive Projects.

This book is written in a modular format and provides exercises after reviewing each major topic. Topics are introduced in an order that is consistent with most object-oriented C++ textbooks. As a result, instructors and students should find it easy to use this book as a supplement to any primary text. The exercises make excellent lab assignments, and you can use the end-of-chapter projects as programming assignments.

Features

Developing Projects Using Object-Oriented C++ includes the following superior features:

- The **"Read This Before You Begin" Page** illustrates Course Technology's unequaled commitment to helping instructors introduce technology into the classroom. Technical considerations and assumptions about hardware and software are listed in one place to help instructors save time and eliminate unnecessary aggravation.
- **Exercises** are included for each major section of the book. They focus students on developing new applications; modifying existing programs to add functionality, improve methods of storing data, or reorganize the programs; and debugging existing programs.
- **Examples** are used throughout each chapter to illustrate how to use the C++ programming language to write object-oriented programs.
- A **Summary** at the end of each chapter recaps the programming concepts and commands covered in that chapter.
- Each chapter concludes with two **Progressive Projects** and two **Independent Projects** that deal with contemporary topics. Multiple projects give instructors and students flexibility in their choice of programming challenges.
  - *Progressive Projects*   The two Progressive (continuing) Projects that students develop using the concepts reviewed in the chapter are complete applications. These projects are designed to allow students to develop C++ programs incrementally.
  - *Independent Projects*   The two Independent Projects do not build upon work completed in a previous chapter. Instead, these smaller projects ask students to create smaller applications to solve smaller problems.

Software

This book was written to be compiler-independent. While differences exist in the interfaces used by different compilers, the C++ code itself is standard. All example programs, exercises, and projects were tested using Microsoft Visual C++, version 5.0, and Inprise C++, version 5.0. In a UNIX environment, the only change needed in the C++ code affects the method used to specify a full path-name for a file. (The instructor's disk contains UNIX student files.)

Acknowledgments

I would like to thank all of the people who helped to make this book possible, especially Jessica Evans, my Developmental Editor, who offered me encouragement, patience, humor, and flexibility when I needed it. Her expertise has made this text a better book. Thanks also to Kristen Duerr, Associate Publisher; Cheryl Ouellette, Product Manager; and Margarita Donovan, Associate Product Manager, for their patience, support, and flexibility. Thanks also to Ellina Beletsky, Production Editor; Jill E. Hobbs, Copyeditor; and Nicole Ashton, Quality Assurance tester.

I am grateful to the many reviewers who provided helpful and insightful comments during the development of this book, including Albert E. Cawns, Webster University; Richard J. Coppins, Virginia Commonwealth University; Joseph F. Laiacona, Columbia College Chicago; Joan Ramuta, University of St. Francis; and Suzanne Sever, Wayne State College.

Finally, I would like to dedicate this book to Sugar, my constant companion as I wrote this book.

Jo Ann Smith

Contents

Read This Before You Begin

To the Student

Student Disks

To complete the exercises and projects in this book, you need Student Disks. Your instructor will provide you with student files. When you begin each chapter, make sure you are using the correct Student Disk.

Using Your Own Computer

You can use your own computer to complete the exercises and projects in this book. To do so, you will need a C++ compiler. This book was written so you can use any C++ compiler to complete the exercises and projects. The programs in this book were written and tested using the Microsoft Visual C++, version 5.0 compiler, as well as the Inprise C++, version 5.0 compiler. If you are using Microsoft Visual C++, you must compile your programs from your hard drive, because Visual C++ creates large intermediate files in the compilation process, which will not fit on a floppy disk. If you are using the Inprise compiler, however, then the exercises and projects for this book will fit on a single high-density floppy disk.

Most of the example programs and exercises in this book require you to compile multiple .ccp files to create the single executable file that contains your application. Chapter 1 contains a review of typical C++ object-oriented program organization techniques. Ask your instructor or consult the documentation for your specific compiler for information about compiling multiple files.

To the Instructor

To complete the chapters in this book, your students must use a set of student files. You must be a registered adopter of this book to receive these files. Follow the instructions in the Help file to copy the student files to your server or stand-alone computer. You can view the Help file using a text editor such as WordPad or Notepad.

Once the files are copied, you can make Student Disks for the students yourself, or tell students where to find the files so they can make their own Student Disks. If your students are using the Microsoft Visual C++, version 5.0 compiler, then they must compile their programs from a hard drive—the student files will not compile correctly on a floppy disk. In this case, students can read data files from drive A. UNIX users should use the UNIX student files on the instructor's disk so the files will compile properly.

Course Technology Student Files

You are granted a license to copy the student files to any computer or computer network used by students who have purchased this book.

Introduction to Object-Oriented Concepts and C++ Classes

Introduction▶ Chapter 1 assumes that you have learned C++ syntax and concepts in a previous class. In this chapter, you will review the concepts of abstraction and data encapsulation. You also will create a class, data members, and methods (member functions); make class members `public` or `private`; create an object; and use simple classes in a C++ program. Finally, you will review the organization of C++ program files.

Object-Oriented Programming

If you are a procedural programmer, becoming an object-oriented programmer requires you to think about writing programs in a different way. To design procedural programs, you decompose a large problem into smaller problems until you can solve the smaller problems. You then write a C++ function to solve each of the smaller problems. If the function requires data from another location in your program, you must pass that data to the function as arguments. Figure 1-1 illustrates the relationship between data and the functions that print data in a procedural program.

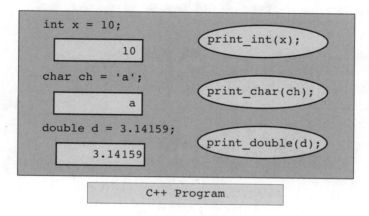

Figure 1-1: Relationship between data and functions in procedural programming

As you can see in Figure 1-1, the data and functions remain separate. The programmer creates the relationship between the two by passing the data to the function. Procedural programming places the main focus on the tasks that your code will execute. Thus procedural programs comprise a sequence of actions that specify what the computer should do.

Object-oriented programming is another way of thinking about programming. Here the focus is on the relationship between data and tasks, rather than on a program's tasks. In object-oriented programming, a program contains objects that respond to messages sent to them. A **message** (**function call**) is simply a request for the object to do something. In C++, you create objects that contain data and actions or behaviors that the object is capable of performing. You implement these actions, called **methods** (or member functions), by writing functions that are part of the object itself. Figure 1-2 illustrates the relationship between data and methods in object-oriented programming.

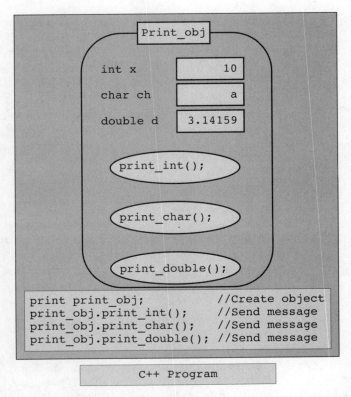

Figure 1-2: Relationship between data and methods in object-oriented programming

As you can see in Figure 1-2, the relationship between the data and methods is built into the object itself. After you create the object named `print_obj`, it knows how to `print_int()`, `print_char()`, and `print_double()`. Data are not passed to these methods; rather, the object knows how to print the values of the data members that belong to the same object. For example, the C++ statement `print_obj.print_char();` sends the `print_char()` message to the `print_obj` object. The `print_obj` object responds by printing the character stored in its `char` data member.

Data Encapsulation

An object-oriented language must provide support for data encapsulation. **Data encapsulation** refers to the process of hiding or encapsulating data within an object. In object-oriented programming, data and the functions that operate on that data are part of a single item, which is referred to as an object. The data are called **data members** and the functions are called methods (or member functions). The details of the implementation (data) are encapsulated within the class, which means the data are hidden from the class's users by keeping the data inaccessible to them. Instead, the class's users must use one of the methods. The methods have direct access to the data because the data are encapsulated or hidden in the class.

Because C++ supports data encapsulation, changes made to the representation of the data members will affect only the methods of the class. Although the class author might need to rewrite the methods to accommodate the changes to the representation of the data, you do not need to change programs that were written using the class. That's because the user of the class—a programmer—used the class interface (methods) and did not worry about the implementation details.

Abstractions

You can create abstractions to solve complex problems. An **abstraction** has an interface that provides the means to use the abstraction by defining which operations might be performed or by defining how a programmer might use the abstraction. In this way, the abstraction provides access to the implementation.

An abstraction also has an implementation. The details of the implementation remain hidden from the abstraction's user, who interacts with the implementation details by using the interface. Figure 1-3 illustrates one such abstraction, involving the automobile.

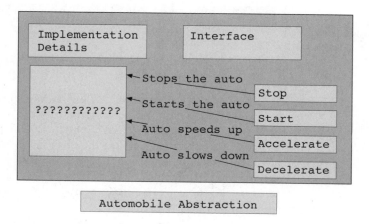

Figure 1-3: Automobile abstraction

When you use an automobile, you instruct it to start by inserting the key in the ignition and turning it; this process defines how to use the automobile interface to start the car. You do not have to understand all the details of how your car actually starts to understand how to use the interface.

The same is true for accelerating, decelerating, and stopping your car. You step on the gas pedal to accelerate to a new speed. You press the brake pedal to slow the car to a reduced speed. To stop the car, you push the brake pedal until the car decelerates to zero miles per hour. You do not need to understand how the engine or other components of an automobile work to accomplish these actions; you need to understand only how to use the automobile's interface (the gas and brake pedals). The same idea holds true for using abstractions in programming. You do not need to understand the internal workings of an abstraction; you just need to use the abstraction's interface correctly.

As stated earlier, procedural programs consist of a sequence of actions that specify what the computer should do. **Procedural abstractions** are created to model these actions. In procedural programming, you can write functions as abstractions. Procedural abstractions allow many users to use the procedure without understanding its implementation details. You use procedural abstractions when you use library functions, such as the square root function. For example, to use the C++ square root function, you need to know the following information, which collectively defines the interface that a programmer must use:

- The purpose of the function
- The number of arguments, and the data types of those arguments, that are passed to the function
- The value returned by the function and the return value's data type

In contrast, you create abstract data types (or data abstractions) in object-oriented programming. You might think of an **abstract data type** as a new, user-defined data type. The abstract data type allows programmers to use the abstraction without knowing its underlying implementation details. You already use abstractions when you use any of the built-in C++ data types, such as float, double, int, and char. When you create and use variables in a C++ program, you are not concerned about how C++ implements them; you simply use the operations that are defined for that particular data type. For example, you can add or subtract floats or use the modulus operator with an int. C++ allows programmers to create classes (user-defined data types) that are abstract data types.

Exercise 1.1 ▶ Choose one of the following abstractions and, on a piece of paper, write a description of its interface: a microwave oven, a video cassette recorder (VCR), or an elevator.

Classes

Syntax ▶

```
class Class_name
{
  public:
    public member declarations;
  private:
    private member declarations;
}; // NOTE: The semicolon is needed.
```

In C++, you implement an abstract data type as a class. You specify the interface and the implementation details as part of the class definition. After you create the class definition, you can instantiate—that is, create an instance of—the class. An instance of a class is called an **object**. You can consider the class definition to be a template that C++ uses to create objects. When you create an object, it contains a collection of data members (implementation details) and methods (member functions that define the interface).

The syntax for defining a class is similar to structure syntax. By convention, you begin the name of a class with a capital letter in C++.

Public and Private Sections

A class can include three sections: public, private, and protected. You will learn about protected sections in Chapter 5.

In the **public section**, you define the class's interface. The public section is the part of the class that will be available to the class's users or to programmers who will create objects of this class type in their C++ programs. It lists the methods that belong to the class. These methods define the behaviors or operations that you can use to work with objects of the class type.

In the **private section** of a class, you specify the class's implementation details. You usually place data members in the private section. These private data members are not directly accessible to a class's users. Instead, they can be accessed only by using the methods provided for the class. Example 1-1 shows the class definition for a `Video` class.

Example 1-1 ▶

```
// video.h

const int SIZE = 40;

class Video
{
  public:
    Video();
    void set_all(char*, char*, short);
    const char* get_name();
    const char* get_producer();
    short get_quantity();
  private:
    char name[SIZE];
    char producer[SIZE];
    short quantity;
};  // You must end the class definition with a semicolon!
```

The `Video` class has three private data members (`name`, `producer`, and `quantity`) in the private section of the class, and five public methods (`Video()`, `set_all()`, `get_name()`, `get_producer()`, and `get_quantity()`) in the public section of the class. The `get_name()` and `get_producer()` methods both return a constant pointer to a character because `name` and `producer` are both private data members. Returning a constant pointer to a character ensures that the data cannot be accessed through the pointer.

If the class definition does not include the keyword `public` or `private`, then the class members will be `private` by default.

Exercise 1.2 ▶

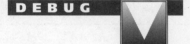

The class definition for the `Employee` class is as follows:

```cpp
// employee.h
const int NAME_LEN = 40;
const int SSN_LEN = 20;

class Employee
{
  public:
    // Default constructor; discussed in next section
    Employee();
    // Assigns values to private data members
    void set_all(char*, char*, double);

    // Returns value of private data member, name
    const char* get_name();

    // Returns value of private data member, ssn
    const char* get_ssn();

    // Returns value of private data member, salary
    double get_salary();
  private:
    char name[NAME_LEN];
    char ssn[SSN_LEN];
    double salary;
};
```

On a piece of paper, modify the class definition to add the following data members: `age`, `phone`, and `office_number`. Then add the following methods: `get_age()`, `get_phone()`, and `get_office()`. Also modify the `set_all()` method to accommodate the new data members.

Exercise 1.3 ▶

The following is the class definition for the `Date` class. On a piece of paper, identify and correct the errors in this code.

```cpp
// date.h
class Date
{
  public:
    Date();
    int get_month();
    int get_day()
    int get_year();
    void set_all(int; int; int)

    int month;
    int day;
    int year;
}
```

Exercise 1.4 ▶

On a piece of paper, write the class definition for a `Paycheck` class, which contains the following data members: check number, employee name, date of check, net pay, gross pay, federal tax withheld, state tax withheld, and Social Security tax withheld. The `Paycheck` class should have the following methods:

■ `set_all()`: This function takes arguments for seven of the eight data members (net pay is the exception) and assigns values to them.

- `calc_pay()`: This function calculates the net pay and assigns the calculated value to the net pay data member. Net pay is calculated as the gross pay minus federal, state, and Social Security taxes.
- `get` functions: Declare a `get` function for each data member. For example, the `get_check_num()` method should return the value of the `check_number` private data member using the following function declaration: `int get_check_num();`.

Creating an Object

Syntax ▶	`Class_Name object_name;`

Creating an object resembles the process of creating a variable. Example 1-2 shows a statement that creates an object named `rental`. The `rental` object has the `Video` class type and, therefore, contains the `Video` class data (`name`, `producer`, and `quantity`). The `rental` object also contains a default constructor (`Video()`), and four behaviors or operations defined for this object: `get_name()`, `get_producer()`, `get_quantity()`, and `set_all()`.

Example 1-2 ▶	`Video rental;`

Defining Methods

After you write the class definition, you must write the methods. Writing a method is similar to writing any other C++ function.

Syntax ▶	`return_type Class_name::method_name(argument list)`
	`{`
	  `// Statements that make up the method`
	`}`

Scope Resolution Operator (::) You use the **scope resolution operator**, which is written as two colons (::), when you define methods so as to associate a method name with a class. The scope resolution operator is required because it enables C++ to identify the class to which the method you are defining belongs. Example 1-3 shows the function definitions for the methods of the `Video` class.

Example 1-3 ▶

```cpp
// video.cpp

#include "video.h"
#include <string.h>

// The default constructor is discussed in the next section
void Video::set_all(char* v_name, char* prod, short qty)
{
  strcpy(name, v_name);
  strcpy(producer, prod);
  quantity = qty;
}

const char* Video::get_name()
{
  return name;
}

const char* Video::get_producer()
{
  return producer;
}

short Video::get_quantity()
{
  return quantity;
}
```

Because `set_all()`, `get_name()`, `get_producer()`, and `get_quantity()` are methods of the `Video` class, they have access to the private data members of the `Video` class (that is, `name`, `producer`, and `quantity`). The `set_all()` function is the only method that accepts arguments. Therefore, the `set_all()` function also has access to its arguments (that is, `v_name`, `prod`, and `qty`).

Defining a Default Constructor

A **constructor** is a class method that performs initialization of an object. Constructors are called automatically whenever you create an object; they guarantee that the object will be initialized correctly. Unlike other methods, constructors are not called explicitly using the name of the object. In fact, you cannot explicitly call a constructor; rather, it is called automatically. The constructor itself does not allocate memory. Instead, the compiler allocates memory for the object and then automatically gives control to a constructor to perform the initialization. If you do not write a constructor for a class, C++ will allocate memory for the object, but will not initialize that memory, so the object will not be initialized properly.

The **default constructor** is a constructor written with no arguments. (You will learn about other types of constructors in Chapter 2.) When you write a constructor, you name it using the same name as the class to which it belongs; you do not specify a return data type. You should place constructor declarations in the class definition and include their definitions in the same file with the definitions of the other methods.

Example 1-4 shows the rewritten `Video` class, which includes a default constructor. A `print()` method that prints the values of the three private data members has been added as well.

Example 1-4 ▶

```cpp
// video.h
const int SIZE = 40;
class Video
{
  public:
    Video();  // Default constructor
    void set_all(char*, char*, short);
    void print();
    const char* get_name();
    const char* get_producer();
    short get_quantity();
  private:
    char name[SIZE];
    char producer[SIZE];
    short quantity;
};

// video.cpp
#include "video.h"
#include <iostream.h>
#include <string.h>

// Default constructor, invoked with no arguments;
// initializes all data members to 0 values.
Video::Video()
{
  strcpy(name,"");
  strcpy(producer, "");
  quantity = 0;
}

void Video::print()
{
  cout << name << producer << quantity << endl;
}
// Other methods are written here
```

Exercise 1.5 ▶

The following program duplicates the `set_all()` method for the `Employee` class that you used in Exercise 1.2. This method was written before you added the data members `phone`, `office_number`, and `age`. On a piece of paper, modify the `set_all()` method to accommodate the additional data members and write a default constructor.

```cpp
#include "employee.h"
#include <string.h>

void Employee::set_all(char* nm, char* ssnumber, double sal)
{
  strcpy(name, nm);
  strcpy(ssn, ssnumber);
  salary = sal;
}
```

Exercise 1.6 ▶

The following program duplicates the class definition and the method definitions for the `Date` class. On a piece of paper, identify and correct the errors in this code.

```cpp
class Date
{
  public
    Date()
    set_month(int);
    set_day(int);
    set_year(int);
    print_date()

    int month;
    int day;
    int year;
}

void Date::Date()
{
  month = 0;
  day = 0;
  year = 0;
};
int set_month(int mnth);
{
  month = mnth;
}

void set_day(dy)
{
  day = dy;
};

void set_year(int yr)
{
  yr = year;
}

void print_date()
{
  cout << day << '/' << month << '/' << yr << endl;
};
```

Exercise 1.7 ▶

DEVELOP

On a piece of paper, write the class definition and the method definitions for a `Bank_Account` class. The `Bank_Account` class should have the following data members: `name`, `account_number`, `balance`, and `interest_rate`. It should also have the following methods:

- `Bank_Account()`: This function is the default constructor.
- `deposit()`: This function is passed an amount to deposit and subsequently adjusts the balance.
- `withdraw()`: This function is passed an amount to withdraw and subsequently adjusts the balance.
- `calc_interest()`: This function calculates the simple interest on the account by using the interest rate and balance data members and subsequently adjusts the balance by adding the interest.
- `get_name()`: This function returns the name.
- `get_account()`: This function returns the account number.
- `get_balance()`: This function returns the balance.
- `get_interest()`: This function returns the interest rate.

- set_all(): This function is passed a name, account number, balance, and interest rate and assigns these arguments to the private data members of the class.

Invoking a Method

You use an object's name to invoke or call methods. Example 1-5 shows how to invoke the set_all() method using the object named rental.

Example 1-5 ▶

```
rental.set_all(video_name, producer_name, qnty);
```

The object used to call a method is called the **invoking object**. Methods have access to the private members of the invoking object. When you invoke the set_all() method by using the rental object, the method copies the values of the function arguments (video_name, producer_name, and qnty) into the private data members of the rental object (name, producer, and quantity, respectively).

Figure 1-4 shows the rental object before and after the default constructor is automatically invoked and after a programmer explicitly invokes the set_all() method.

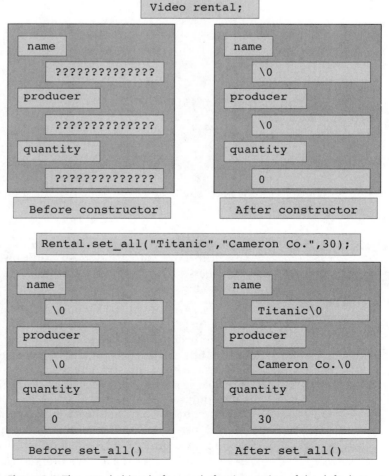

Figure 1-4: The rental object before and after invocation of the default constructor and the set_all() method

Exercise 1.8 ▶

On a piece of paper, write C++ statements to create an object of the Employee class. (This Employee class is the same one used in Exercises 1.2 and 1.5.) After you create the Employee class object, use it to invoke the methods that are part of the Employee class. Invoke each method at least once.

Writing a C++ Program Using a Class

In a C++ program, you can create objects and then use them to invoke the methods of the class to which they belong. Example 1-6 shows a C++ program that uses objects that belong to the Video class.

Example 1-6 ▶

```cpp
// Ex1-6.cpp

#include "video.h"
#include <iostream.h>

int main()
{
  // Two objects are created
  // Default constructor is automatically invoked twice
  Video vid_item1, vid_item2;

  // vid_item1 object invokes methods of the Video class
  vid_item1.set_all("Titanic", "Cameron Co.", 40);
  cout << vid_item1.get_name() << endl;
  cout << vid_item1.get_producer() << endl;
  cout << vid_item1.get_quantity() << endl;

  // vid_item2 object invokes methods of the Video class
  vid_item2.set_all("As Good As It Gets", "Jack's, Inc.", 30);
  cout << vid_item2.get_name() << endl;
  cout << vid_item2.get_producer() << endl;
  cout << vid_item2.get_quantity() << endl;

  return 0;
}
```
Output:
```
Titanic
Cameron Co.
40
As Good As It Gets
Jack's, Inc.
30
```

Organization of Object-Oriented C++ Programs

Programmers usually organize the files in an object-oriented C++ program as follows:

- The class definition appears in a header file that is given the same name as the class. For example, the Video class definition appears in a file named video.h.

- The definitions of class methods appear in a file that has the same name as the class, but with a .cpp extension. For example, the method definitions for the `Video` class are placed in a file named video.cpp. You `#include` the header file, video.h, in this file.
- The C++ program that uses the `Video` class appears in an appropriately named .cpp file. For example, the program shown in this chapter that uses the `Video` class is stored in a file named Ex1-6.cpp. You `#include` the header file, video.h, in this file.

You must compile both .cpp files to create a single executable program file. Ask your instructor or consult the documentation for your specific compiler for information about compiling multiple files.

Remember to use the C++ preprocessor directive `#ifndef` to avoid including the header file multiple times in your final program. If you include a header file more than once in a C++ program, it will result in a compile-time error. You can use the conditional compilation statement, `#ifndef`, to avoid multiple inclusions of header files. Example 1-7 shows a header file that includes conditional compilation statements.

Example 1-7 ▶

```
// video.h
#ifndef VIDEO_H
#define VIDEO_H
const int SIZE = 40;
class Video
{
  public:
    Video();  // Default constructor
    void set_all(char*, char*, short);
    void print();
    const char* get_name();
    const char* get_producer();
    short get_quantity();
  private:
    char name[SIZE];
    char producer[SIZE];
    short quantity;
};
#endif
```

In Example 1-7, the preprocessor interprets the `#ifndef` statement as follows:

If the symbolic constant VIDEO_H is not defined then
  Define the symbolic constant VIDEO_H
  Include the contents of the header file in the source code file.

When the preprocessor encounters additional statements to `#include` the video.h file, the `#ifndef VIDEO_H` statement will be false because `VIDEO_H` is already defined. As a result, the contents of the header file will not be included in the file.

Exercise 1.9 ▶

The Chapter1 folder on your Student Disk contains the following files: the class definition for the Time class is saved as time.h, the Time class methods are saved as time.cpp, and a C++ program that uses the Time class is saved as Ch1-9.cpp. Study the contents of these three files and then make the following modifications:

- Add a default constructor.
- Add a set_all() method that assigns values to the three data members hour, minute, and second.
- Create a third Time object in your C++ program and invoke the set_all() method with the third object.
- When you are finished, save the modified files as timea.h, timea.cpp, and Ch1-9a.cpp in the Chapter1 folder.

Exercise 1.10 ▶

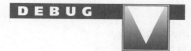

The Chapter1 folder on your Student Disk contains the following files: the class definition for the Rectangle class is saved as rectangle.h, the Rectangle class methods are saved as rectangle.cpp, and a C++ program that uses the Rectangle class is saved as Ch1-10.cpp. The program calculates the area and perimeter of a rectangle. Because the program does not compile, however, you don't know if it calculates these values correctly. Find and fix the errors so that the program will run and produce the correct output. When you are finished, save the corrected files as rectanglea.h, rectanglea.cpp, and Ch1-10a.cpp in the Chapter1 folder.

Exercise 1.11 ▶

The Chapter1 folder on your Student Disk contains the following files: the class definition for the Video class is saved as video.h, and the Video class methods are saved as video.cpp. The Video class is similar to the Video class used throughout this chapter, with a few changes. Study this Video class and then write a C++ program that uses it. Your C++ program should create three Video objects. Populate the objects with data read in from the file named video.dat in the Chapter1 folder. Use the new update_quantity() method to update the quantity data member of the three Video objects. Prompt the user to enter the number of videos received, and then use that value to update the quantity for all three Video objects. Next, use the new get_quantity() method to display the quantities of the three Video objects before and after updating the quantities. Finally, display the values stored in the three objects. When you are finished, save your C++ program in a file named Ch1-11a.cpp in the Chapter1 folder.

Using an Array of Objects

You can create and use an array of objects employing the same techniques you use to create and use an array of integers, doubles, floats, or characters. Example 1-8 shows the C++ code that creates an array of Video objects and then invokes the methods of the Video class using the Video objects stored in the array.

Example 1-8 ▶

```
// Ex1-8.cpp

#include "video.h"
#include <string.h>
#include <iostream.h>

const int NUM_ITEMS = 10;
const int A_SIZE = 30;
```

```
int main()
{
  Video vid_items[NUM_ITEMS];
  char vid_name[A_SIZE];
  char vid_prod[A_SIZE];
  short qnty;
  int k;

  for(k = 0; k < NUM_ITEMS; k++)
  {
    cout << "Enter the name of the video: ";
    cin.getline(vid_name, A_SIZE);
    cout << "Enter the producer's name: " ;
    cin.getline(vid_prod, A_SIZE);
    cout << "Enter the quantity: ";
    cin >> qnty;
    vid_items[k].set_all(vid_name,vid_prod,qnty);
    cin.ignore(256,'\n');  //Flush newline
  }

  for(k = 0; k < NUM_ITEMS; k++)
  {
    cout << "Video Name: " << vid_items[k].get_name() << endl;
    cout << "Producer: " << vid_items[k].get_producer() << endl;
    cout << "Quantity: " << vid_items[k].get_quantity() << endl;
  }

  return 0;
}
```

Exercise 1.12

In Exercise 1.9, you modified the class definition for the `Time` class and a C++ program that used the `Time` class. In this exercise you will again modify that C++ program (Ch1-9a.cpp) so as to create and use an array of 10 `Time` objects, with the same messages being sent to each object in the array as were sent to the `Time` objects in the original program. The class definition for the `Time` class is saved as time.h and the class methods are saved as time.cpp in the Chapter1 folder. When you are finished, save the modified program as Ch1-12a.cpp in the Chapter1 folder.

Exercise 1.13

The program saved as Ch1-13.cpp in the Chapter1 folder on your Student Disk includes some modifications to the program you debugged in Exercise 1.10. This program calculates the area and perimeter of rectangle objects, but now you have created an array of `Rectangle` objects. Because your program does not compile, you don't know if it calculates the areas and perimeters correctly. The class definition for the `Rectangle` class is saved as rectangle.h and the `Rectangle` class methods are saved as rectangle.cpp in the Chapter1 folder. Find and fix the errors so that the program will run and produce the correct output. When you are finished, save the corrected file as Ch1-13a.cpp in the Chapter1 folder.

Exercise 1.14 ▶

Write a C++ class for an airplane. The `Airplane` class should have three data members: type of airplane, current flying speed, and maximum flying speed. The class should have the following methods:

- `Airplane()`: The default constructor.
- `set_type()`: Assigns a value to the type of airplane data member.
- `set_current_speed()`: Assigns a value to the current flying speed data member.
- `set_max_speed()`: Assigns a value to the maximum flying speed data member.
- `get_type()`: Returns the type of airplane.
- `get_current_speed()`: Returns the current speed.
- `get_max_speed()`: Returns the maximum speed.

Write a C++ program that creates two `Airplane` objects and then invokes methods to fly the planes at a particular speed. Use `cout` statements to announce the speed of the airplane. Assign a maximum speed to your `Airplane` objects to prevent an airplane from flying faster than its maximum speed. When you are finished, save your class definition as airplane.h, your class method definitions as airplane.cpp, and your program as Ch1-14a.cpp in the Chapter1 folder on your Student Disk.

S U M M A R Y

- To write object-oriented C++ programs you must change the way you think about programming. Object-oriented programs focus on the relationship between data and tasks, rather than on tasks alone.
- An object-oriented program consists of objects that respond to messages.
- A message is a request for an object to perform some action.
- Objects contain both data and methods. Methods define the behaviors or operations that an object is capable of performing.
- A class consists of data members and methods. The data members define the implementation details of the class, and the methods define the operations or behaviors.
- An object is an instance of a class. When you create an object, it contains data and can respond to messages that direct the object to perform certain operations.
- A class includes public, private, and protected sections. Data members are included in the private section, and methods usually appear in the public section.
- Members in the private section are not accessible to the users (or programmers) of the class. Private members remain hidden from the class's users and are encapsulated within the class. Access to the private members occurs through the public members.
- Members in the public section of a class define the class's interface. Class users must use the interface when interacting with the class. Public members have access to the private members.
- An abstraction allows you to focus on only essential items to solve a complex problem. It includes an interface and an implementation. The implementation defines the details and remains hidden from the user. The interface provides the means to use the abstraction by defining which operations are allowed.
- Procedural abstractions allow many users to use a procedure without understanding the details of its implementation.

- A class is an abstract data type or a user-defined type in C++. Programmers can use abstract data types without knowing the underlying implementation details. Each abstract data type includes an interface that programmers use to gain access to the implementation details that are encapsulated within the class.

- Class definitions include the class name, private members, and public members. Data members are specified with a name and a data type. Method declarations include the return type of the method, the method name, and the data types of arguments passed to the method.

- The process of defining methods is similar to defining any function in C++, but you also include the scope resolution operator, which identifies the class to which the method belongs.

- Methods are invoked or called using an object.

- You write object-oriented C++ programs by creating objects and then invoking their methods.

- You can create and use an array of objects using the same techniques employed to create and use an array of a built-in data type.

PROGRESSIVE PROJECTS

You will complete one or both of the Progressive Projects as you work through this book by adding more functionality in each successive chapter. Eventually, you will complete the projects by using object-oriented programming techniques and C++.

1. Green Grocery Online Shopping

In this project, you will simulate an online grocery-shopping program. When shopping online, customers can choose various grocery items and have them delivered to their homes without actually visiting the store itself. Your program will modify the grocery store inventory when a customer places a grocery item in a virtual grocery cart. It will maintain a running total of each customer's bill and will display this tally at the customer's request. It also will print the customer's order for review before delivering the order to the customer's address.

In this chapter, you will create a `GroceryItem` class that contains the following data: `item_name`, `item_price`, `quantity_on_hand`, and `qty_purchased`. The `GroceryItem` class will contain the following methods:

- `GroceryItem()`: The default constructor.
- `set_item_name()`: Assigns a value to the data member `item_name`.
- `set_item_price()`: Assigns a value to the data member `item_price`.
- `set_qty_on_hand()`: Assigns a value to the data member `quantity_on_hand`.
- `set_qty_purchased()`: Sets `qty_purchased` to zero before a customer begins shopping.
- `get_item_name()`: Returns the value of the data member `item_name`.
- `get_item_price()`: Returns the value of the data member `item_price`.
- `get_qty_on_hand()`: Returns the value of the data member `quantity_on_hand`.
- `get_qty_purchased()`: Returns the value of the data member `qty_purchased`.

Write a C++ program that creates an array of 10 `GroceryItem` objects. Open the data file saved as grocery.dat in the Chapter1 folder on your Student Disk, and read the data from this file and assign values to the 10 `GroceryItem` objects. Next, display these items to allow a customer to select grocery items from the list and indicate the quantity of that item he or she would like to order. When the customer finishes shopping, the program should display the items and quantities he or she has chosen, calculate the total bill, and then simulate delivering the order with a `cout` statement that announces the customer's total bill and tells the customer that the order will be delivered by the end of the day.

When you are finished, save your program as Ch1-pp1.cpp and your class files as grocery.h and grocery.cpp in the Chapter1 folder on your Student Disk.

2. Modified Five-Card Stud Poker

In this project, you will simulate four people playing the game of modified five-card stud poker without betting. When playing this modified version of five-card stud, the dealer gives five cards, one at a time, to each player. After the players receive their five cards, the winning hand is determined.

Players will use a deck of cards that contains 52 cards. The deck includes four suits: hearts, diamonds, spades, and clubs. Each suit has 13 cards: Ace (high), King, Queen, Jack, 10, 9, 8, 7, 6, 5, 4, 3, and 2.

Your program will determine a winning hand based on Figure 1-5. The first hand in the list is the best hand.

Hand	Description
Straight flush	Five cards of the same suit and in sequence—for example, K Q J 10 9 of hearts. The hand with the highest "high" card is the winning flush.
Four of a kind	Four cards of the same kind—for example, four 7s.
Full house	Two cards of the same kind and three cards of another kind—for example, 5 5 5 3 3.
Flush	Five cards with the same suit—for example, 2 5 8 10 K of spades.
Straight	Five cards in sequence of any suit—for example, 2 of spades, 3 of hearts, 4 of clubs, 5 of diamonds, 6 of spades.
Three of a kind	Three cards of the same kind—for example, three 5s.
Two pairs	Two cards of the same kind and two cards of another kind—for example, two 4s and two 8s.
One pair	Two cards of the same kind—for example, two 7s.
High card	Highest card in the player's hand.

Figure 1-5

In this section, you will create a `Card` class that contains the data and methods shown in Figure 1-6.

Data	
suit	Hearts, diamonds, spades, clubs.
type	14 (Ace), 13 (King), 12 (Queen), 11 (Jack), 10, 9, 8, 7, 6, 5, 4, 3, 2.
used	1 when a card has been dealt; 0 when a card has not been dealt.
Methods	
`Card()`	Default constructor.
`set_suit()`	Assigns a value to the suit data member.
`set_type()`	Assigns a value to the type data member.
`set_used()`	All cards are assigned the value 0 before the game begins.
`get_suit()`	Returns the value of the suit data member.
`get_type()`	Returns the value of the type data member.
`get_used()`	Returns the value of the used data member.

Figure 1-6

Write a C++ program that creates an array of 52 `Card` objects and four arrays of 5 `Card` objects to represent the deck and the four player's hands. Assign values to each of the 52 `Card` objects by assigning values that are read from the input file saved as card.dat in the Chapter1 folder on your Student Disk. Next, deal five cards each to four poker players. Use a random number between 0 and 51 to determine which card in the array the program should deal. After dealing the card, use the `set_used()` method to mark the card as "used." The same card should not be dealt more than once in the same game. After dealing five cards to each player, display each player's hand. In the next chapter, you will create constructors and a destructor for the `Card` class and change the implementation of data members. When you are finished, save your program as Ch1-pp2.cpp and your class files as card.h and card.cpp in the Chapter1 folder on your Student Disk.

INDEPENDENT PROJECTS

1. Bird Watchers

The Beautiful Birds Society has asked you to write a program to manage information on the location and time of sightings for various birds. Create a `Sighting` class to manage the following data for each bird: bird type, sighting date, sighting location, and bird watcher's name. The user should be able to enter data and list all of the information for all birds. When you are finished, save your program as Ch1-ip1.cpp and your class files as sighting.h and sighting.cpp in the Chapter1 folder on your Student Disk. Use the following date as your input:

Bird Type	Sighting Date	Sighting Location	Bird Watcher
Eastern Bluebird	8/28/99	Glen Ellyn Woods	Natalie Johnson
Red Winged Blackbird	8/30/99	Waterfall Glen	Tom Egan
Brown Nuthatch	10/4/99	Fox River Park	Kim Hashoien

2. Automobiles

Write a C++ program that simulates driving an automobile. Create an `Automobile` class that contains the following data: auto type, current speed, and maximum speed. You should be able to start, stop, accelerate, decelerate, steer, turn on your left and right blinkers, and make a right or left turn. When you are finished, save your program as Ch1-ip2.cpp and your class files as auto.h and auto.cpp in the Chapter1 folder on your Student Disk.

Writing Class Methods

Introduction ▶ In this chapter, you will review the following topics that relate to the methods you provide for a class: understanding polymorphism, overloading functions, overloading operators, using default function arguments, and creating constructors and destructors. In addition, you will learn about the system-supplied pointer named `this`.

Introduction to Polymorphism

To be object-oriented, a programming language must provide support for data encapsulation, polymorphism, and inheritance. You already have seen how C++ supports data encapsulation; you will learn about inheritance in Chapter 4.

The word *polymorphism* comes from two Greek words: *poly*, meaning "many", and *morph*, meaning "form." A **polymorphic function**, therefore, is a function that takes many forms. The simplest form of polymorphism in C++ is the ability to overload functions, as you will see next.

Overloading Functions

You can **overload** functions by giving the same name to more than one function. C++ allows you to overload methods defined for a class as well as functions that are not part of a class.

When you define functions and give them the same name, you must give the functions a different number of arguments, give them different argument data types, or make them members of different classes. C++ uses a function's signature to determine which overloaded function it should call. A function's **signature** consists of the function name and the argument list, but not the function's return type. C++ will also try to match a function's signature by using standard type conversions; for example, it can convert an integer argument to a double.

Function overloading is possible because C++ performs **name mangling**, which means that it automatically changes the name of an overloaded function from just the function's name to a combination of the function's name and the arguments. One benefit of overloading is that the programmer has the ability to give meaningful names to functions, rather than making up different names for several functions that perform exactly the same task but work on different data types.

Example 2-1 shows the function definitions of four overloaded functions named **product()** that differ in terms of the number of arguments or the data type of their arguments. These functions are not part of a class.

Example 2-1 ▶

```
int product(int value1, int value2)
{
  return value1 * value2;
}
int product(int value1, int value2, int value3)
{
  return value1 * value2 * value3;
}
double product(double value1, double value2)
{
  return value1 * value2;
}
double product(double value1, double value2, double value3)
{
  return value1 * value2 * value3;
}
```

Exercise 2.1 ▶ Match each function declaration to each function call. Specify #1, #2, #3, or #4 on the lines provided.

```
//Function declarations

#1  int product(int,int);
#2  int product(int,int,int);
#3  double product(double,double);
#4  double product(double,double,double);


// Function calls
double num1 = 1.0, ans1;
int num2 = 5, ans2;
_____   ans2 = product(2,5);
_____   ans1 = product(num1,2.0,5.0);
_____   ans1 = product(num1,num1);
_____   ans1 = product(2,5.0);
_____   ans1 = product(2,4,num1);
_____   ans2 = product(3,5,7);
```

Example 2-2 shows the class definition for the Video class, which contains four overloaded methods named set_all(). It also shows the definitions for the set_all() methods.

Example 2-2 ▶

```cpp
// video.h
#ifndef VIDEO_H
#define VIDEO_H
const int SIZE = 40;
class Video
{
  public:
    Video();  // Default constructor
    void set_all();  // No arguments
    void set_all(char*);  // One argument
    void set_all(char*, char*);  // Two arguments
    void set_all(char*, char*, short);  // Three arguments

    const char* get_name();
    const char* get_producer();
    short get_quantity();
  private:
    char name[SIZE];
    char producer[SIZE];
    short quantity;
};
#endif
```

```cpp
// Contents of file named video.cpp
#include "video.h"
#include <string.h>

// Invoked with no arguments;
// assigns 0 values to all data members.
void Video::set_all()
{
  strcpy(name,"");
  strcpy(producer, "");
  quantity = 0;
}


// Invoked with one argument (the video name);
// assigns name_in to the name data member
// and assigns 0 values to the other data members.

void Video::set_all(char* name_in)
{
  strcpy(name, name_in);
  strcpy(producer, "");
  quantity = 0;
}


// Invoked with two arguments (the video name and the
// producer name); assigns 0 to the quantity data member.

void Video::set_all(char* name_in, char* prod_in)
{
  strcpy(name, name_in);
  strcpy(producer, prod_in);
  quantity = 0;
}


// Invoked with three arguments (the video name,
// producer name, and quantity).

void Video::set_all(char* name_in, char* prod_in, short qty)
{
  strcpy(name, name_in);
  strcpy(producer, prod_in);
  quantity = qty;
}
```

Exercise 2.2 ▶ Match each method declaration to each invocation. Specify #1, #2, #3, or #4 on the lines provided.

```cpp
// video.h
#ifndef VIDEO_H
#define VIDEO_H
const int SIZE = 40;
```

```
class Video
{
  public: Video();   // Default constructor
    void set_all();                          // #1
    void set_all(char*);                     // #2
    void set_all(char*, char*);              // #3
    void set_all(char*, char*, short);  // #4

    const char* get_name();
    const char* get_producer();
    short get_quantity();
  private:
    char name[SIZE];
    char producer[SIZE];
    short quantity;
};
#endif


// overloaded.cpp
#include <iostream.h>
#include "video.h"
int main()
{
  Video vid_item1, vid_item2, vid_item3, vid_item4;
  vid_item1.set_all();                                        // _____
  vid_item2.set_all("Titanic", "Cameron Co.", 56);  // _____
  vid_item3.set_all("Titanic");                             // _____
  vid_item4.set_all("Titanic", "Cameron Co.");         // _____
  // Rest of program
  return 0;
}
```

Default Function Arguments

In C++, you can assign default values to function arguments. Later, if you do not provide actual arguments in an invocation, C++ will use these default values, thereby eliminating the need for some overloaded functions. The default values for the arguments appear in the function declaration/prototype. When creating default values, remember that all arguments do not need default values; once you specify a default value for an argument, however, all subsequent arguments must have a default value as well.

In Example 2-3, the Video class has been rewritten so that the four set_all() methods are replaced with a single method that uses default function arguments. The default values for the name and producer are the null string. The default value for quantity is zero. To run the following example program, you must compile two files—video.ccp and Ex2-3.ccp—to create a single executable file.

Example 2-3 ▶

```
// video.h
#ifndef VIDEO_H
#define VIDEO_H
const int SIZE = 40;
class Video
{
```

```
    public:
      Video();  // Default constructor
      // set_all() method declaration with default arguments
      void set_all(char* = "", char* = "", short = 0);
      const char* get_name();
      const char* get_producer();
      short get_quantity();
    private:
      char name[SIZE];
      char producer[SIZE];
      short quantity;
};
#endif


// Ex2-3.cpp
#include "video.h"
int main()
{
  Video vid1;
  // Uses all 3 default argument values
  vid1.set_all();
  // Uses 2 default argument values
  vid1.set_all("Titanic");
  // Uses 1 default argument value
  vid1.set_all("Titanic", "Cameron Co.");
  // Uses 0 default argument values
  vid1.set_all("Titanic", "Cameron Co.", 56);
  return 0;
}
```

Exercise 2.3 ▶

In Chapter 1, you used the Time class in several exercises. In this exercise, you will modify the Time class to replace the set methods with one method named set_values(). The set_values() method should use default function arguments so that all data members will be initialized regardless of whether you supply values to the method. The Chapter2 folder on your Student Disk contains the following files: the Time class definition is saved as time.h, the methods are saved as time.cpp, and the C++ program named Ch2-3.cpp enables you to test your modified class. Save your modified files as timea.h and timea.cpp.

Exercise 2.4 ▶

The Chapter2 folder on your Student Disk contains the following files: the House class definition is saved as house.h, the methods for this class are saved as house.cpp, and the program named Ch2-4.cpp uses the House class to manage information about several homes that you are interested in purchasing. This program does not compile correctly. Study these three files, find and fix the errors, and then run the program again. Save your corrected files as housea.h, housea.cpp, and Ch2-4a.cpp in the Chapter2 folder.

Exercise 2.5 ▶

Create a CD class and its class methods so that you can enter the name, recording artist, and cost of a music CD. Next, write a C++ program that uses the CD class to store and print the information about 10 of your favorite CDs. Your solution should use overloaded functions and/or default function arguments. Save the CD class definition as cda.h, your method definitions as cda.cpp, and your program as Ch2-5a.cpp in the Chapter2 folder on your Student Disk.

Constructors and Destructors

A **constructor** is a class member that initializes an object, and a **destructor** is a class member that performs clean-up activities for an object.

Constructor Functions

Constructors are called automatically whenever an object is created. They guarantee that the object will be initialized correctly. A constructor is called when *any* of the following conditions occur:

- An `automatic`, `static`, or `external` storage class object is created.
- A temporary object is needed (for example, automatic type conversions).
- An object is created on the heap using dynamic memory allocation.
- An object is created by copying an existing object.
- An object is passed by value into or returned from a function.

Unlike other methods, constructors are not called explicitly using the name of an object. In fact, you cannot explicitly call a constructor; it is called automatically for you. You can overload constructors, which allows you to create and initialize objects in multiple ways. As you learned in Chapter 1, a constructor that takes no arguments is known as the **default constructor**. A constructor itself does not allocate memory. Instead, the compiler allocates memory for the object, and then automatically gives control to a constructor to perform the initialization. If you do not write a constructor for a class, C++ allocates memory for the object, but the memory and object are not initialized properly.

When writing constructors, you give the constructor the same name as the class to which it belongs, and you do not specify a return data type. You should place constructor declarations in the class definition and write their definitions in the same file with the definitions of the other methods.

Example 2-4 shows the rewritten `Video` class. Three additional constructors have been added as well as a `print()` method that prints the values of the three private data members. To run the following example program, you must compile two files—video.ccp and Ex2-4.ccp—to create a single executable file.

Example 2-4 ▶

```cpp
// video.h
#ifndef VIDEO_H
#define VIDEO_H
const int SIZE = 40;
class Video
{
  public:
    Video();  // Default constructor
    Video(char*);  // One argument
    Video(char*, char*);  // Two arguments
    Video(char*, char*, short);  // Three arguments

    void set_all(char* = "", char* = "", short = 0);
    void print();
    const char* get_name();
    const char* get_producer();
    short get_quantity();
  private:
    char name[SIZE];
    char producer[SIZE];
```

```cpp
    short quantity;
};
#endif

// video.cpp
#include <iostream.h>
#include <string.h>
#include "video.h"

// Default constructor, invoked with no arguments;
// initializes all data members to 0 values.

Video::Video()
{
  strcpy(name,"");
  strcpy(producer, "");
  quantity = 0;
}

// Invoked with one argument (the video name); initializes
// name with the value of name_in and initializes other
// data members to 0 values.

Video::Video(char* name_in)
{
  strcpy(name, name_in);
  strcpy(producer, "");
  quantity = 0;
}

// Invoked with two arguments (the video name and the
// producer name); initializes quantity to 0.

Video::Video(char* name_in, char* prod_in)
{
  strcpy(name, name_in);
  strcpy(producer, prod_in);
  quantity = 0;
}

// Invoked with three arguments (the video name,
// producer name, and quantity).

Video::Video(char* name_in, char* prod_in, short qty)
{
  strcpy(name, name_in);
  strcpy(producer, prod_in);
  quantity = qty;
}
void Video::print()
{
  cout << name << " " << producer << " " << quantity;
  cout << endl;
}
```

```
  // Other methods are written here

  // Ex2-4.cpp
  #include <iostream.h>
  #include "video.h"
  int main()
  {
    // Default constructor is invoked automatically
    Video vid_item1;
    // Constructor that expects three arguments
    // is invoked automatically.
    Video vid_item2("Titanic", "Cameron Co.", 56);
    // Constructor that expects one argument
    // is invoked automatically.
    Video vid_item3("Titanic");
    // Constructor that expects two arguments
    // is invoked automatically.
    Video vid_item4("Titanic", "Cameron Co.");

    vid_item1.print();
    vid_item2.print();
    vid_item3.print();
    vid_item4.print();
    // Rest of program
    return 0;
  }
```

Output:

```
0
Titanic Cameron Co. 56
Titanic 0
Titanic Cameron Co. 0
```

A constructor function is called automatically when you use the new operator to create an object on the heap. When objects are dynamically allocated, you must use the -> operator to invoke methods because the new operator returns a pointer. Example 2-5 illustrates the use of the new operator to create several objects that would result in the automatic invocation of one of the overloaded constructors, followed by the use of the pointers and the -> operator to invoke the print() method. To run the following example program, you must compile two files—video.ccp and Ex2-5.ccp—to create a single executable file.

Example 2-5 ▶

```
// video.h
#ifndef VIDEO_H
#define VIDEO_H
const int SIZE = 40;
class Video
{
  public:
    Video();  // Default constructor
    Video(char*); // One argument
    Video(char*, char*);  // Two arguments
    Video(char*, char*, short);  // Three arguments
```

```
      void set_all(char* = "", char* = "", short = 0);
      void print();
      const char* get_name();
      const char* get_producer();
      short get_quantity();
   private:
      char name[SIZE];
      char producer[SIZE];
      short quantity;
};
#endif


// Ex2-5.cpp
#include <iostream.h>
#include "video.h"
int main()
{
  // Default constructor is invoked automatically
  Video* vid_ptr1 = new Video;
  // Constructor that expects three arguments
  // is invoked automatically.
  Video* vid_ptr2 = new Video("Titanic", "Cameron Co.", 56);
  // Constructor that expects one argument
  // is invoked automatically.
  Video* vid_ptr3 = new Video("Titanic");
  // Constructor that expects two arguments
  // is invoked automatically.
  Video* vid_ptr4 = new Video("Titanic", "Cameron Co.");
  // Use pointers to invoke the print() method
  vid_ptr1->print();
  vid_ptr2->print();
  vid_ptr3->print();
  vid_ptr4->print();
  // Rest of program
  return 0;
}
```

Output:

```
0
Titanic Cameron Co. 56
Titanic 0
Titanic Cameron Co. 0
```

Exercise 2.6 ▶

Modify the Time class again (see Exercise 2.3) so that the class definition contains all of the constructors it needs to ensure that objects of the Time class are initialized properly. Place a cout statement in each constructor to verify that it has been called in your program. The Chapter2 folder on your Student Disk contains the following files: the Time class definition is saved as time1.h, the methods are saved as time1.cpp, and the C++ program named Ch2-6.cpp enables you to test your modified class. Save your modified files as time1a.h and time1a.cpp in the Chapter2 folder.

Exercise 2.7 ▶

You wrote a C++ program that uses a `Date` class. You included all of the methods and constructors needed to ensure the proper initialization and use of the `Date` class. Your program does not work properly; in fact, it does not even compile. Study the three relevant files—date.h, date.cpp, and Ch2-7.cpp—in the Chapter2 folder on your Student Disk to find the errors. Fix the errors so that the program runs successfully. Save the corrected files as datea.h, datea.cpp, and Ch2-7a.cpp in the Chapter2 folder.

Exercise 2.8 ▶

Write an `Email` class and a C++ program that uses this class. The `Email` class should allow you to keep track of people to whom you have sent important e-mail messages and the date and time at which you sent these messages. For each message, your program should store the recipient's name, a short description of the message's topic, and the date (month, day, and year) and time (hour, minute, and second) that the message was sent. Your program should allow you to enter this information for five e-mail messages and then print the information for each message. Make sure that you write all necessary constructors for the `Email` class. Save the class definition as emaila.h, the methods as emaila.cpp, and the C++ program as Ch2-8a.cpp in the Chapter2 folder on your Student Disk.

Copy Constructor

The **copy constructor** is a special constructor that is invoked when an object is created and initialized with the values stored in the data members of an existing object. The copy constructor is called when any of the following events occur:

- A new object is created using an existing object.
- An object is passed by value to a function.
- An object is returned from a function.

If you do not write a copy constructor, C++ will provide one for your class; sometimes, however, the copy constructor supplied by C++ may not be adequate. It will perform a **member-wise copy**, which means that the compiler will copy the data from each data member in one object to another object. When your class includes pointer data members, the member-wise copy will only duplicate pointers, which will result in two objects with pointers to the same memory space. If the destructor is called for one of the objects, the dynamically allocated memory is released. If the other object later refers to that storage, it will result in an error. To avoid this problem, you should write your own copy constructor to ensure that memory is allocated correctly. For example, if the existing object stores a pointer to the video named "L.A. Confidential," then the copy constructor must allocate enough memory to store this name in the new object. The copy constructor always takes one argument, a constant reference to a class object.

Example 2-6 shows the `Video` class with a copy constructor added. The implementation used to store the video's name and producer has been changed as well. Now, both `name` and `producer` are pointers; the actual storage for these pointers is dynamically allocated. The change in implementation requires changes in the default constructor and other constructors. Example 2-6 shows these rewritten constructors. It is important to understand that when the implementation of the data members changes, you might need to rewrite the methods; as long as the interface remains unchanged, however, you need not rewrite programs that use this class. To run the following example program, you must compile two files—video.ccp and Ex2-6.ccp—to create a single executable file.

Example 2-6 ▶

```cpp
// video.h
#ifndef VIDEO_H
#define VIDEO_H
class Video
{
  public:
    Video();  // Default constructor
    Video(char*);  // One argument
    Video(char*, char*);  // Two arguments
    Video(char*, char*, short); // Three arguments
    Video(const Video&);  // Copy constructor

    void set_all(char* = "", char* = "", short = 0);
    void print();
    const char* get_name();
    const char* get_producer();
    short get_quantity();
  private:
    // name is now a pointer to a character
    char* name;
    // producer is now a pointer to a character
    char* producer;
    short quantity;
};
#endif

// video.cpp
#include <iostream.h>
#include <string.h>
#include "video.h"

// Default constructor, invoked with no arguments;
// initializes all data members to 0 values.

Video::Video()
{
  // Allocate memory to store the null string in
  // name and producer.
  name = new char[strlen("") + 1];
  producer = new char[strlen("") + 1];
  strcpy(name,"");
  strcpy(producer, "");
  quantity = 0;
}

// Invoked with one argument (the video name); initializes
// name with the value of name_in and initializes other
// data members to 0 values.

Video::Video(char* name_in)
{
  // Allocates memory to store the video name passed in
  name = new char[strlen(name_in) + 1];
```

```cpp
  strcpy(name, name_in);
  // Allocates memory to store the null string
  producer = new char[strlen("") + 1];
  strcpy(producer, "");
  quantity = 0;
}


// Invoked with two arguments (the video name and the
// producer name); initializes quantity to 0.

Video::Video(char* name_in, char* prod_in)
{
  // Allocates memory to store the video name
  name = new char[strlen(name_in) + 1];
  strcpy(name, name_in);
  // Allocates memory to store the producer name
  producer = new char[strlen(prod_in) + 1];
  strcpy(producer, prod_in);
  quantity = 0;
}


// Invoked with three arguments (the video name,
// producer name, and quantity).

Video::Video(char* name_in, char* prod_in, short qty)
{
  // Allocates memory to store the video name
  name = new char[strlen(name_in) + 1];
  strcpy(name, name_in);
  // Allocates memory to store the producer name
  producer = new char[strlen(prod_in) + 1];
  strcpy(producer, prod_in);
  quantity = qty;
}
// Copy constructor; invoked when a new object is created
// by initializing it with the values stored in an
// existing object.
Video::Video(const Video& video_in)
{
  // Allocates memory to store the video name
  name = new char[strlen(video_in.name) + 1];
  strcpy(name, video_in.name);
  // Allocates memory to store the producer name
  producer = new char[strlen(video_in.producer) + 1];
  strcpy(producer, video_in.producer);
  quantity = video_in.quantity;
}
void Video::print()
{
  cout << name << " " << producer << " " << quantity << endl;
}
// Other methods are written here
```

```cpp
// Ex2-6.cpp
#include "video.h"
int main()
{
  // Initialization using the default constructor
  Video vid1;
  // Initialization using the constructor that expects
  // one argument.
  Video vid2("As Good As It Gets");
  // Creating a new object from an existing object; uses
  // the copy constructor.
  Video vid3 = vid2;
  // Creating a new object on the heap using the default
  // constructor.
  Video* vid4 = new Video;
  // Creating an array of three Video objects; calls the
  // default constructor three times.
  Video vid_array[3];
  vid1.print();
  vid2.print();
  vid3.print();
  vid4->print(); // Uses pointer returned by new operator
  for(int i = 0; i < 3; i++)
    vid_array[i].print();
  delete vid4;
  return 0;
}
```

Output:

```
0
As Good As It Gets 0
As Good As It Gets 0
0
0
0
0
```

Exercise 2.9

Modify the Time class again by adding a copy constructor for the class. You can use the Time class definition that is saved as time2.h and the methods that are saved as time2.cpp in the Chapter2 folder on your Student Disk, or you can use the Time class files you created in Exercise 2.6 (time1a.h and time1a.cpp). Use the C++ program saved as Ch2-9.cpp in the Chapter2 folder to test your modified class. Save your modified files as time2a.h and time2a.cpp.

Exercise 2.10

You are writing a Book class to manage your personal library. The following files are saved in the Chapter2 folder on your Student Disk: the Book class definition is saved as book.h, and the methods for the Book class are saved as book.cpp. Your C++ program (Ch2-10.cpp) reads in your book data from the file named book_info.dat and stores the data in an array of Book objects, and then prints a list of books that are priced at less than $20. This program will not compile, however. Find and fix the errors so that it runs and produces the correct output. Save your corrected files as booka.cpp, booka.h and Ch2-10a.cpp in the Chapter2 folder.

Exercise 2.11 ▶

Write a C++ program that simulates a dice game. Write a `Dice` class so you can create two objects in your program that represent the two dice you will throw. Write the methods and constructors needed to initialize a `Dice` object correctly and determine the value thrown for each die. Your program should save and then report the results for 10 dice throws. Save your class definition as dicea.h, the methods as dicea.cpp, and your C++ program as Ch2-11a.cpp in the Chapter2 folder on your Student Disk.

Constructor Initialization Lists

Constructors often contain several assignment statements to initialize an object. You also can initialize an object by using initialization lists. Technically, a constructor should initialize objects rather than assign values. If a class contains data members that are constants, the constructor must use an initialization list because you cannot assign values to a constant. You also use initialization lists when working with inheritance; you will learn about inheritance in Chapters 4 and 5. To use initialization lists, in the method definition you type a colon after the argument list and then enclose in parentheses a comma-delimited list of data members with initial values. Example 2-7 shows the `Video` class constructor that takes three arguments rewritten using an initialization list.

Example 2-7 ▶

```
Video::Video(char* name_in, char* prod_in, short qty):
  name(name_in), producer(prod_in), quantity(qty)
{
  // No code needed
}
```

The body of the constructor shown in Example 2-7 is empty because you no longer need the assignment statement and the `strcpy()` functions that previously appeared in the body.

Destructors

A destructor executes when an object is destroyed. It is responsible for "cleaning up," but not for freeing the memory allocated for the object. It manages any memory that was dynamically allocated by the object's constructors. The destructor is called under the following conditions:

- After `main()`, when static and external objects go out of scope.
- After each block containing local, automatic objects.
- After each function that has been passed an object by value.
- When a dynamically allocated object is destroyed using the `delete` operator.
- When temporary objects are destroyed.

Writing destructors is not always necessary. In fact, you need to write a destructor only for any class that uses dynamic memory allocation for its data members. Because you altered the implementation of the `Video` class to include two data members (`name` and `producer`) that are pointers, and the memory to store the names of the video and producer is dynamically allocated, you must write a destructor for the `Video` class.

To write a destructor, you give it the same name as the class and precede that name with a tilde (~). Destructors, like constructors, are written without specifying a return data type. They take no arguments and you cannot overload them like constructors. You place the destructor declaration in the class definition and its definition in the .cpp file with the other methods.

Example 2-8 shows the destructor for the Video class.

Example 2-8 ▶

```cpp
Video::~Video()
{
  // Frees memory that was dynamically allocated
  // in the constructor.
  delete [] name;
  // Deletes memory that was dynamically allocated
  // in the constructor.
  delete [] producer;
}
```

The C++ program in Example 2-9 illustrates how a destructor is called. To run the following example program, you must compile two files—video_1.h and Ex2-9.ccp—to create a single executable file.

Example 2-9 ▶

```cpp
// Ex2-9.cpp
#include "video_1.h"
int main()
{
  // Initialization using the default constructor
  Video vid1;
  // Initialization using the constructor that expects
  // one argument.
  Video vid2("As Good As It Gets");
  // Creates a new object from an existing object;
  // uses the copy constructor.
  Video vid3 = vid2;
  // Creates a new object on the heap using the default
  // constructor.
  Video* vid4 = new Video;
  // Creates an array of three Video objects; calls the
  // default constructor three times.
  Video vid_array[3];
  // Prints values of data members
  vid1.print();
  vid2.print();
  vid3.print();
  // Uses the -> operator because vid4 is a pointer
  vid4->print();
  for(int i = 0; i < 3; i++)
    vid_array[i].print();
  delete vid4;  // Destructor called once
  return 0;
  // Destructor called six times
}
```

Output:

```
0
As Good As It Gets 0
```

```
As Good As It Gets 0
0
0
0
0
In Video destructor.
In Video destructor.
In Video destructor.
In Video destructor.
In Video destructor.
In Video destructor.
In Video destructor.
```

Exercise 2.12 ▶

The Student class definition is saved as student.h, the methods for the Student class are saved as student.cpp, and a C++ program that uses this Student class is saved as Ch2-12.cpp in the Chapter2 folder on your Student Disk. Modify the Student class so that the student name is no longer stored in an array of characters; it should instead be implemented as a pointer to a character and you should dynamically allocate the memory to store the name. Because of this change in implementation, you must change some of the existing methods and constructors and write a destructor for the Student class. Do not change the Ch2-12.cpp program. Instead, save your modified files as studenta.h and studenta.cpp in the Chapter2 folder.

Exercise 2.13 ▶

You wrote a C++ program to manage your class schedule this semester. In the process, you created a Course class and wrote the methods, constructors, and a destructor for the Course class, which are saved as course.h and course.cpp in the Chapter2 folder on your Student Disk. Your program, Ch2-13.cpp, creates five Course objects and prompts you to enter data to store in each one. After receiving data for the five objects, your program should print your schedule. The current version of your program compiles but does not run. Find and fix the errors so that it generates the correct output. Save your corrected files as coursea.h and coursea.cpp in the Chapter2 folder.

Exercise 2.14 ▶

The WriteRight Publishing Company has asked you to develop a program to track sales data for its published books. Write a C++ program that uses an array of 10 Textbook objects. Populate the Textbook objects with the following data saved in a file named text_info.dat in the Chapter2 folder on your Student Disk: book name, author last name, author first name, ISBN number, price, number sold (this month), and number sold (year to date). After the data are entered, your program should print a report listing the book name, total sales this month (in dollars), and total year-to-date sales (in dollars) for each book. Save your Textbook class definition as textbooka.h, the methods as textbooka.cpp, and the C++ program as Ch2-14a.cpp in the Chapter2 folder on your Student Disk.

Operator Overloading

C++ allows you to overload operators as part of a class definition. If you overload an operator for a class, it will use your user-defined overloaded operator with objects of that class type. If the operator has not been overloaded for a class, using the operator with objects of that class type will result in an error, because C++ will attempt to use the built-in operator and will not know how to use the operator with a user-defined type.

The Equality Operator: operator==()

Overloaded operators always have the name **operator***op*, where *op* stands for a built-in C++ operator. For example, a function named operator==() is an overloaded operator that overloads the equality operator (==). You can overload any C++ operator except the . operator, the ?: operator, the .* operator, the :: operator, and the sizeof operator. The overloaded operator must use the same number of operands as the built-in operator, and you cannot change the precedence or the associativity of the built-in operator. In addition, you cannot create new operators or change the meaning of the operators for the built-in data types.

The overloaded operator is invoked when you use the operator symbol in a C++ program with objects as operands. The following code illustrates the use of the overloaded == operator with Video objects as operands.

```
if(video1 == video2)
```

When C++ encounters the overloaded operator ==, the two objects are used as follows: The object to the left of the operator is considered the invoking object, and the object on the right of the operator is passed to the operator==() function as an argument. Therefore, the statement in the previous code sample is equivalent to the following C++ statement:

```
video1.operator==(video2);
```

The value returned from an overloaded operator is the value of the expression. For example, the operator==() function returns a value of 1 (true) or 0 (false).

To include the overloaded operator as part of the Video class, you must modify the class definition. Example 2-10 shows the modified Video class definition.

Example 2-10 ▶

```
// video.h
#ifndef VIDEO_H
#define VIDEO_H
class Video
{
  public:
    Video();  // Default constructor
    Video(char*);  // One argument
    Video(char*, char*);  // Two arguments
    Video(char*, char*, short);  // Three arguments
    Video(const Video&);  // Copy constructor
    ~Video();  // Destructor

    int operator==(Video&);  // Overloaded == operator
    void set_all(char* = "", char* = "", short = 0);
    void print();
    const char* get_name();
    const char* get_producer();
    short get_quantity;
  private:
    // name is now a pointer to a character
    char* name;
    // producer is now a pointer to a character
    char* producer;
    short quantity;
};
#endif
```

In Example 2-10, the class definition now includes the function declaration for the overloaded operator `operator==()`. The `operator==()` function returns an `int` (`true` or `false`) and expects one argument: a reference to the `Video` object on the right side of the operator. The `Video` object on the left side of the operator is the invoking object.

Now you must write the definition for the `operator==()` function. You add the overloaded operator `operator==()` definition to the video.cpp file where the other methods are stored. Example 2-11 shows the definition for the overloaded operator, `operator==()`.

Example 2-11 ▶

```
// video.cpp
#include "video.h"
// Other method definitions
// Overloaded equality operator
int Video::operator==(Video& rhs)
{
  if(!(strcmp(name, rhs.name)) &&
    !(strcmp(producer, rhs.producer)) &&
    quantity == rhs.quantity)
    return 1;  // They are the same
  else
    return 0;  // They are not the same
}
```

The Assignment Operator: `operator=()`

When the assignment operator (=) is overloaded for the `Video` class, C++ statements such as `video1 = video2;` should copy all of the data members from the `video2` object to the data members of the `video1` object.

Assignment expressions return the value assigned to the variable on the left side of the assignment operator. To maintain consistency, when you overload the assignment operator for a class, you should create an `operator=()` function that returns a reference to the object on the left side of the operator. For example, the statement `video1 = video2;` must return a pointer (or a reference) to `video1`, which can be accomplished by returning `*this` from the `operator=()` function. C++ supplies the `this` pointer, where `this` always points to the invoking object. In the statement `video1 = video2;`, the object on the left side of the operator (`video1`) is the invoking object and `video2` is the object passed to the `operator=()` function. Therefore, the value of `this` is the address of the `video1` object and the value of `*this` is the `video1` object (that is, the invoking object).

Example 2-12 shows the modified video.h file in which the overloaded operator `operator=()` has been added to the `Video` class definition.

Example 2-12 ▶

```
// video.h
#ifndef VIDEO_H
#define VIDEO_H
class Video
{
  public:
    Video();  // Default constructor
    Video(char*);  // One argument
```

```
Video(char*, char*); // Two arguments
Video(char*, char*, short);  // Three arguments
Video(const Video&);  // Copy constructor
~Video();  // Destructor

// Overloaded equality operator
int operator==(Video&);
// Overloaded assignment operator
Video& operator=(Video&);
void print();
const char* get_name();
const char* get_producer();
short get_quantity();
private:
// name is now a pointer to a character
char* name;
// producer is now a pointer to a character
char* producer;
short quantity;
};
#endif
```

Example 2-13 shows the definition for the overloaded operator operator=( ) that was added to the video.cpp file where the other methods are stored.

Example 2-13 ▶

```
// video.cpp
#include "video.h"
// Other method definitions
// Overloaded assignment operator
Video& Video::operator=(Video& rhs)
{
  if(this == &rhs)  // Don't do it, it is the same object
    // Return a reference to the object on the left side
    return *this;
  else
  {
    // Free previously allocated memory
    delete [] name;
    delete [] producer;
    // Allocate memory for the new name and producer
    name = new char[strlen(rhs.name) + 1];
    producer = new char[strlen(rhs.producer) + 1];
    // Copy strings and short from rhs to the invoking object
    strcpy(name,rhs.name);
    strcpy(producer, rhs.producer);
    quantity = rhs.quantity;
    // Return a reference to the object on the left side
    return *this;
  }
}
```

Example 2-14 shows a C++ program that uses the overloaded operator `operator==()` and the overloaded operator `operator=()`. To run the following example program, you must compile two files—video.ccp and Ex2-14.ccp—to create a single executable file.

Example 2-14 ▶

```
// Ex2-14.cpp
#include "video.h"
#include <iostream.h>
int main()
{
Video rent1("As Good As It Gets", "Jack's Inc.", 30);
Video rent2;
Video rent3 = rent1; // Invokes the copy constructor
rent2 = rent1;       // Invokes operator=()
if(rent1 == rent2)   // Invokes operator==()
  cout << "The two objects are the same." << endl;
else
  cout << "The two objects are not the same." << endl;
  return 0;
}
Output:
The two objects are the same.
```

Overloaded Math Operators

You also can overload the math operators (that is, + – * /). For example, if you want to overload these operators for the `Video` class, first you must define what it means to add, subtract, multiply, or divide two `Video` objects. Some of these operations might not make sense, so you probably would not want to overload an unreasonable operator for the `Video` class. If you decide to add two `Video` objects (meaning to calculate a total of the two quantities), you would add the overloaded operator `operator+()` declaration to the video.h file and add the overloaded operator `operator+()` definition to the video.cpp file. Example 2-15 shows these modifications as well as a C++ program that uses the newly overloaded + operator. To run the following example program, you must compile two files—video.ccp and Ex2-15.ccp—to create a single executable file.

Example 2-15 ▶

```
// video.h
#ifndef VIDEO_H
#define VIDEO_H
class Video
{
  public:
    Video();  // Default constructor
    Video(char*);  // One argument
    Video(char*, char*);  // Two arguments
    Video(char*, char*, short);  // Three arguments
    Video(const Video&);  // Copy constructor
    ~Video();  // Destructor

    int operator==(Video&);  // Equality operator
    Video& operator=(Video&);  // Assignment operator
    short operator+(Video&);  // Overloaded + operator
```

```
    void set_all(char* = "", char* = "", short = 0);
    void print();
    const char* get_name();
    const char* get_producer();
    short get_quantity;
  private:
    // name is now a pointer to a character
    char* name;
    // producer is now a pointer to a character
    char* producer;
    short quantity;
};
#endif

// video.cpp
// Other method definitions
// Overloaded addition operator
short Video::operator+(Video& rhs)
{
  short total;
  total = quantity + rhs.quantity;
  return total;
}

// Ex2-15.cpp
#include "video.h"
#include <iostream.h>
int main()
{
  Video rent1("Titanic", "Cameron Co.", 56);
  Video rent2("As Good As It Gets", "Jack's Inc.", 32);
  short total_qty;
  // Invokes the operator+() function
  total_qty = rent1 + rent2;
  cout << "There are " << total_qty << " copies in stock."
    << endl;
  return 0;
}
```

Output:

```
There are 88 copies in stock.
```

Overloading ++ and −−

You also can overload the C++ increment and decrement operators. First, you must decide what it means to increment and decrement a Video object. For example, you might decide that incrementing a Video object adds 1 to the quantity on hand. Then you add the declaration to the class definition and add the definition to the .cpp file that contains the class methods and overloaded operators. Example 2-16 shows the modified class definition, which now includes the overloaded operator operator++(). The declaration for operator++(), its definition, and a C++ program that uses the overloaded ++ operator appear in Example 2-16. To run the following example program, you must compile two files—video.ccp and Ex2-16.ccp—to create a single executable file.

Example 2-16 ▶

```cpp
// video.h
#ifndef VIDEO_H
#define VIDEO_H
class Video
{
  public:
    Video();  // Default constructor
    Video(char*);  // One argument
    Video(char*, char*);  // Two arguments
    Video(char*, char*, short);  // Three arguments
    Video(const Video&);  // Copy constructor
    ~Video();  // Destructor

    int operator==(Video&);  // Equality operator
    Video& operator=(Video&);  // Assignment operator
    // Overloaded + operator
    short operator+(Video&);
    // Overloaded ++ operator (prefix)
    Video& operator++();
    void print();
    const char* get_name();
    const char* get_producer();
    short get_quantity();
  private:
    // name is now a pointer to a character
    char* name;
    // producer is now a pointer to a character
    char* producer;
    short quantity;
};
#endif

// video.cpp
// Other method definitions
// Overloaded prefix increment operator
Video& Video::operator++()
{
  ++quantity;
  return *this;
}

// Ex2-16.cpp
#include "video.h"
#include <iostream.h>
int main()
{
  Video rent1("Titanic", "Cameron Co.", 56);
  cout << "There are " << rent1.get_quantity()
    << " copies in stock." << endl;
  ++rent1;
  cout << "There are " << rent1.get_quantity()
    << " copies in stock." << endl;
```

```
        return 0;
    }
```

Output:

```
There are 56 copies in stock.
There are 57 copies in stock.
```

A problem arises when you use the postfix placement of the increment operator because the prefix placement (++rent1) and the postfix placement (rent1++) have different meanings. With the prefix placement, the increment takes place before evaluation of the expression. With the postfix placement, the increment takes place after C++ evaluates the expression. Although you must write a second operator++( ) function, this function will generate an error message if you try to compile a class with two functions having identical signatures. For this reason, you must write the second operator++( ) function that expects a single int argument. The int argument is a **dummy argument**, which means it is never used by the function; it exists only to enable C++ to distinguish between the two functions.

Example 2-17 shows the declaration for the second overloaded operator++( ), added to the class definition in the video.h file, the definition added to the video.cpp file, and a C++ program that uses the two forms of the overloaded operator. To run the following example program, you must compile two files—video.ccp and Ex2-17.ccp—to create a single executable file.

Example 2-17 ▶

```cpp
//  video.h
#ifndef VIDEO_H
#define VIDEO_H
class Video
{
public:
    Video();  // Default constructor
    Video(char*);  // One argument
    Video(char*, char*);  // Two arguments
    Video(char*, char*, short);  // Three arguments
    Video(const Video&);  // Copy constructor
    ~Video();  // Destructor

    int operator==(Video&);  // Equality operator
    Video& operator=(Video&);  // Assignment operator
    // Overloaded + operator
    short operator+(Video&);
    // Overloaded ++ operator (prefix)
    Video& operator++();
    // Overloaded ++ operator (postfix)
    Video& operator++(int);
    void set_all(char* = "", char* = "", short = 0);
    void print();
    const char* get_name();
    const char* get_producer();
    short get_quantity();
private:
    // name is now a pointer to a character
    char* name;
```

```
        // producer is now a pointer to a character
        char* producer;
        short quantity;
};
#endif

// video.cpp
// Other method definitions
Video& Video::operator++()  // Prefix placement
{
  ++quantity;
  return *this;
}
Video& Video::operator++(int)  // Postfix placement
{
  quantity++;
  return *this;
}


// Ex2-17.cpp
#include "video.h"
#include <iostream.h>
int main()
{
  Video rent1("Titanic", "Cameron Co.", 56);
  cout << "There are " << rent1.get_quantity()
    << " copies in stock." << endl;
  ++rent1;
  cout << "There are " << rent1.get_quantity()
    << " copies in stock." << endl;
  rent1++;
  cout << "There are " << rent1.get_quantity()
    << " copies in stock." << endl;
  return 0;
}
```

Output:
```
There are 56 copies in stock.
There are 57 copies in stock.
There are 58 copies in stock.
```

In Chapter 6, you will learn to overload the << (insertion) and >> (extraction) operators. Refer to your primary C++ course textbook for examples of overloading other C++ operators.

Exercise 2.15 ▶

In Exercise 2.12, you modified the Student class. Now you will modify this class again to add the ability to compare one Student object to another. When the name stored in a Student object is the same as the name stored in another Student object, the objects are equal. If the name stored in one Student object is less than the name stored in another Student object, then the former name would appear first in an alphabetically ordered list. If the name stored in one Student object is greater than the name stored in a second Student object, then the former name would appear after the latter name in an alphabetically ordered list. The C++ program saved as Ch2-15.cpp in the Chapter2 folder on your Student Disk uses these comparisons to alphabetize a list of student names before printing each student's final grade. Use this program to test your modified **Student** class. To sort the array of **Student** objects, you must overload the assignment (=) operator. The **Student** class is saved as student1.h, and the methods are saved as student1.cpp in the Chapter2 folder. Save your modified files as student1a.h and student1a.cpp in the Chapter2 folder on your Student Disk.

Exercise 2.16 ▶

The C++ program stored in the file named Ch2-16.cpp in the Chapter2 folder on your Student Disk uses an array of **Salesperson** objects to calculate monthly reimbursement amounts for the number of miles driven in a single month. The += operator has been overloaded for the **Salesperson** class, allowing the program to calculate the total reimbursement amount for all **Salesperson** objects. In its current form, this program does not work correctly. Study the **Salesperson** class definition in sales.h and the method definitions in sales.cpp, and then fix any errors that you find. Do not change the C++ program Ch2-16.cpp. Save your corrected files as salesa.h and salesa.cpp in the Chapter2 folder.

Exercise 2.17 ▶

Write a C++ program that reads in 10 English and 10 French words and stores each English word and its French equivalent in a **Dictionary** object. The English and French words are saved as dict.dat in the Chapter2 folder on your Student Disk. Sort the array of 10 **Dictionary** objects by the English word, and then allow the user to enter an English word and see its French equivalent. Remember to overload the assignment operator for the **Dictionary** class and use dynamic memory allocation to store the words. Save your program as Ch2-17a.cpp, your **Dictionary** class definition as dictionarya.h, and the methods as dictionarya.cpp in the Chapter2 folder on your Student Disk.

SUMMARY

- Polymorphic functions take on many forms. Overloading function names is the simplest form of polymorphism. Function names become overloaded when you write more than one function with the same name.

- C++ uses a function's signature to determine which overloaded function to call. A function's signature includes the function's name and argument list, but not its return type.

- You can overload methods that belong to a class as well as functions that do not belong to a class.

- A benefit of function overloading is that it gives programmers the ability to give meaningful names to all functions that they write.

- You can assign default function arguments in C++. The function uses these default values when actual arguments are not provided.

- A constructor initializes objects of a class type. You can overload constructors to allow for the initialization of objects in multiple ways.

- You do not invoke constructors; rather, they are called automatically immediately after memory is allocated for the object.

- The default constructor does not have any arguments passed to it.

- The copy constructor initializes a new object with the values stored in an existing object. It expects one argument, a constant reference to a class object.

- Initialization lists can be provided for constructors to enable true initialization, rather than using assignment statements in the body of the constructor.

- A destructor is called every time an object is destroyed. It is responsible for "cleaning up." A destructor does not always need to be written, though one should be created if the class constructors dynamically allocate memory for data members. In this case, the destructor is responsible for freeing the memory that was dynamically allocated when the object was created.
- Operators may be overloaded for classes by writing operator*op*() functions, where *op* is the operator symbol.
- You can overload all C++ operators, except the ., ?:, .*, ::, and sizeof operators.
- Overloaded operators have the same precedence and associativity as the built-in operators.
- You cannot change the meaning of operators for the built-in data types or create new operators.
- You cannot change the number of operands required by an operator.

PROGRESSIVE PROJECTS

1. Green Grocery Online Shopping Program

In Chapter 1, you created a GroceryItem class and wrote a C++ program that created an array of 10 GroceryItem objects, gave values to the 10 grocery items, and displayed items available for purchase. You also allowed the customer to choose items and quantities for those items, and you displayed the items the customer purchased, calculated a total bill, and simulated delivering the order using a cout statement announcing that the customer's order was en route.

In this chapter, you will create all necessary constructors for the GroceryItem class by using default function arguments, if appropriate. Also, you should change the implementation of the item_name to use dynamically allocated memory instead of an array of characters. Make sure that you write a destructor for this class, as you are now using dynamically allocated memory. You should also overload the comparison operators (>, <, ==, !=, >=, and <=) so that you can sort the customer's order alphabetically by item_name. In addition, you will need to overload the assignment operator (=).

When you have finished, save your program as Ch2-pp1.cpp and your class files as grocery.h and grocery.cpp in the Chapter2 folder on your Student Disk.

2. Modified Five-Card Stud Poker

In Chapter 1, you created a Card class and then wrote a C++ program that created an array of 52 Card objects to represent the deck, assigned values to each of the 52 cards, and then dealt five cards to four poker players. You used random numbers between 0 and 51 to determine which card in the array to deal. When the program dealt a card, the set_used() method marked the card so that it could not be dealt twice in the same game. After dealing five cards to each player, your program displayed the four players' hands.

In this chapter, you will create all necessary constructors for the `Card` class by using default function arguments, if appropriate. Also, change the implementation of the `suit` data member to use dynamically allocated memory instead of an array of characters. Make sure that you write a destructor for this class, as you are now using dynamically allocated memory. You should also overload the comparison operators (==, >, <, >=, <=, and !=) to make sorting the player's hands easier and eventually to facilitate the identification of the winning hand. Finally, you should sort the players' hands by `card_type` and then display the four players' hands in sorted order.

When you have finished, save your program as Ch2-pp2.cpp and your class files as card.h and card.cpp in the Chapter2 folder on your Student Disk.

INDEPENDENT PROJECTS

1. Bowling

In this project, you will simulate two friends playing a game of bowling. For each of the 10 frames in the game, use the random number generator to determine the number of pins knocked down; store this value in a `Frame` object. In each frame, a player can throw the ball twice. If the player gets a strike (10 pins knocked down) on the first ball, he or she does not need to throw the second ball. You will not keep score as part of this project. Print the results for all 10 frames. Make sure to include the necessary constructors and destructors for the `Frame` class, using default function arguments where appropriate. Save your program as Ch2-ip1.cpp and your class files as frame.h and frame.cpp in the Chapter2 folder on your Student Disk.

2. Post Office

In this project, you will sort envelopes as they arrive at the post office. Your program should sort the envelopes by Zip code and assign them to one of four mail carriers. Zip codes are assigned to mail carriers using the following information:

Mail Carrier	Zip Code
Greg	60515
Natalie	60516
Lynne	60517
Ed	60512

The data for this program are saved in the file named letters.dat in the Chapter2 folder on your Student Disk. This file contains the name of the person to whom the letter is addressed, and the addressee's street address, city, state, and Zip code information. Save your program as Ch2-ip2.cpp and the class files as letter.h and letter.cpp in the Chapter2 folder.

More on Class Methods

Introduction ▶ In this chapter, you will review additional topics related to the methods you write for a class. In particular, you will learn about using friend functions, writing inline functions, including constant data members and constant methods in C++ classes, and including static data members and static methods in C++ classes. You also will review using constant objects and constant arguments.

Friend Functions

Friend functions serve as a connection between unrelated classes and functions. Some functions require access to the private data members of a class, but are not part of the class. Because these functions are not members of the class, however, they do not have access to the private data members. To solve this problem, a class can grant friendship to the following items:

- Nonmember functions (functions not members of any class)
- Methods of another class
- Another class (all methods of the class are friends)

Granting friendship gives the friend access to the private data members of a class. Some experts consider friend functions to be controversial because friendship provides access to the private data that are ordinarily reserved for methods belonging to the class.

Granting Friendship to Nonmember Functions

To grant friendship to a nonmember function, you include the friend's function declaration in the class declaration. Recall that method declarations usually appear in the class declaration's public section. Because friend functions are not members of the class, you do not need to place their declarations in the public section, although they usually appear there. The keyword `friend` distinguishes these functions from methods that belong to the class.

If you declare friend functions in more than one class, the function has access to the private data members of all classes in which the function has been declared as a friend. Functions cannot declare themselves as friends of a class—only the class can grant friendship to the function.

Friend functions are not invoked with an object because they are not members of the class. Because you do not use an invoking object, you cannot use the `this` pointer with friend functions, and friend functions must have an object passed to them as an argument. Passing an object to the friend function provides the needed access to the private data members.

Example 3-1 shows how the `Video` class grants friendship to a `print()` function that displays the name of the video, producer, and quantity on hand for each title. Because the `print()` function is a friend of the `Video` class, it has access to the following private data members of the `Video` class: `name`, `producer`, and `quantity`.

Example 3-1 ▶

```
// video.h
#ifndef VIDEO_H
#define VIDEO_H
class Video
{
  public:
    // Constructor
    Video(char* = "", char* = "", short = 0);
    // Copy constructor
    Video(const Video&);
    // Destructor
    ~Video();
```

```
        // Overloaded operators
        int operator==(Video&);
        Video& operator=(Video&);
        short operator+(Video&);
        Video& operator++();
        Video& operator++(int);

        void set_all(char* = "", char* = "", short = 0);

        const char* get_name();
        const char* get_producer();
        short get_quantity();

        friend void print(Video&); // print() is a friend function
    private:
      char* name;
      char* producer;
      short quantity;
    };
    #endif
```

Writing the C++ code for the body of a friend function is similar to writing other C++ functions, except that the friend function is passed a class object. When you write the friend function definition, you do not write it in the same .cpp file with the class methods. Instead, you place it in a separate .cpp file.

Example 3-2 shows the function definition for the friend function named `print()`.

Example 3-2 ▶

```
// print_one.cpp
#include <iostream.h>
#include "video.h"
void print(Video& video_in)
{
  // Friend function; has access to the private data
  // members of the Video class.
  cout << "Name of Video:   " << video_in.name << endl;
  cout << "Name of Producer:   " << video_in.producer << endl;
  cout << "Quantity on Hand:   " << video_in.quantity << endl;
  return;
}
```

Example 3-3 shows a C++ program that uses the `print()` function as a friend of the `Video` class. In this case, you must compile three files—Ex3-3.cpp, print_one.cpp, and video.cpp—to create a single executable file.

Example 3-3 ▶

```
// Ex3-3.cpp
#include <iostream.h>
#include "video.h"
int main()
{
  Video vid_item1("Titanic", "Cameron Co.", 40);
```

```
Video vid_item2("As Good As It Gets", "Jack's Inc.", 30);
// Using the friend function to print
print(vid_item1);
print(vid_item2);
// Using methods to print
cout << "Name:    " << vid_item1.get_name() << endl;
cout << "Producer:  " << vid_item1.get_producer() << endl;
cout << "Quantity:  " << vid_item1.get_quantity() << endl;
return 0;
}
```

```
Output:
Name of Video:  Titanic
Name of Producer:  Cameron Co.
Quantity on Hand:  40
Name of Video:  As Good As It Gets
Name of Producer:  Jack's Inc.
Quantity on Hand:  30
Name:  Titanic
Producer:  Cameron Co.
Quantity:  40
```

Two or more classes can grant friendship to the same function. For example, if you changed the `print()` function to print information stored in a `Video` object and information about the customer who rented the video that is stored in a `Customer` object, both the `Customer` class and the `Video` class must grant friendship to the `print()` function.

Example 3-4 shows the class declarations for the `Video` class and the `Customer` class. Both classes have granted friendship to the `print()` function. You must write a forward declaration for one of the two classes, because the function declaration for the friend function `print()` is written to accept two arguments: a reference to a `Video` object and a reference to a `Customer` object. As shown in Example 3-4, the function declaration for the `print()` function in the `Customer` class specifies two arguments: a reference to a `Video` object and a reference to a `Customer` object. The compiler will not know about the `Video` class yet because it appears later in the file; this situation causes compiler errors. You use the forward declaration statement to tell the compiler that the `Video` class declaration appears later in the file.

Example 3-4 ▶

```
// video.h
// This file contains the class declaration
// for the Video class and the Customer class.
#ifndef VIDEO_H
#define VIDEO_H
class Video;  // Forward declaration
class Customer
{
  public:  // Other Customer methods
    friend void print(Video&, Customer&);  // Friend function
  private:
    char* name;
    char* address;
    char* phone;
};
```

```
class Video
{
  public:  // Other Video class methods
    friend void print(Video&, Customer&);  // Friend function
  private:
    char* name;
    char* producer;
    short quantity;
};
#endif
```

You need to rewrite the `print()` function definition because it now accepts two arguments. The new function appears in Example 3-5.

Example 3-5 ▶

```
// print_two.cpp
#include <iostream.h>
// Contains Video class and Customer class
#include "video.h"
// The print() function now accepts two arguments
void print(Video& in_video, Customer& in_customer)
{
  cout << "Video Name:   " << in_video.name << endl;
  cout << "Customer Name:   " << in_customer.name << endl;
  cout << "Customer Address:   " << in_customer.address << endl;
  cout << "Customer Phone:   " << in_customer.phone << endl;
  return;
}
```

Example 3-6 shows a C++ program that uses the modified `print()` friend function. In this case, you must compile four files—Ex3-6.cpp, print_two.cpp, video.cpp, and customer.cpp—to create a single executable file.

Example 3-6 ▶

```
// Ex3-6.cpp
#include "video.h" // Contains Video class and Customer class
int main()
{
  Video vid_item("Titanic", "Cameron Co.", 56);
  Customer cust_item("Tom Egan", "111 First St.",
                     "222-222-2222");
  print(vid_item, cust_item);  // Using the friend function
  return 0;
}
```

```
Output:
Video Name:  Titanic
Customer Name:  Tom Egan
Customer Address:  111 First St.
Customer Phone:  222-222-2222
```

Granting Friendship to a Method of Another Class

You also can grant friendship to one or more methods of another class. For example, if you add a query() method to the Customer class, then a Customer object could query the availability for rental of a particular video; the method would return 1 (one) if the video is in stock or 0 (zero) if it is out of stock. The query() method is part of the Customer class and the quantity-on-hand information is private to the Video class, which is not accessible by a Customer class object. If the Video class grants friendship to the query() method in the Customer class, however, then the query() method gains access to the private data members of the Video class. Once again, you need a forward declaration to alert the compiler that it will encounter a class name before the class declaration appears in the file. Example 3-7 shows the class declarations for the Video and Customer classes. The Video class grants friendship to the query() method in the Customer class.

Example 3-7 ▶

```
// video.h
// Contains the Video class and the Customer class
#ifndef VIDEO_H
#define VIDEO_H
class Video;  // Forward declaration
class Customer
{
  public:
    // Other method declarations for the Customer class
    int query(Video&);
  private:
    char* name;
    char* address;
    char* phone;
};

class Video
{
  public:
    // Other method declarations for the Video class
    friend int Customer::query(Video&);
  private:
    char* name;
    char* producer;
    short quantity;
};
```

Example 3-8 shows the definition for the query() method in the Customer class.

Example 3-8 ▶

```
// customer.cpp
// video.h contains the Video class and the Customer class
#include "video.h"
// Other method definitions for the Customer class
```

```
int Customer::query(Video& video_in)
{
  // Accessing a private data member of the Video class
  if(video_in.quantity > 0)
    return 1;
  else
    return 0;
}
```

The C++ program in Example 3-9 uses the `query()` method to access the `quantity` data member of the `Video` object. In this case, you must compile three files—Ex3-9.cpp, video.cpp, and customer.cpp—to create a single executable file.

Example 3-9 ▶

```
// Ex3-9.cpp
// Contains Video class and Customer class
#include "video.h"
#include <iostream.h>
int main()
{
  Video vid_item("Titanic", "Cameron Co.", 3);
  Customer cust1("Natalie Johnson", "222 Second St.",
                 "222-222-2222");
  if(cust1.query(vid_item))  // Friend function
    cout << vid_item.get_name() << " is available." << endl;
  else
    cout << vid_item.get_name() << " is not available.";
  return 0;
}
```

Output:
```
Titanic is available.
```

Granting Friendship to Another Class

You also can grant friendship to an entire class. For example, when the `Video` class grants friendship to the `Customer` class, all of the methods of the `Customer` class gain access to the private data members of the `Video` class.

Example 3-10 shows the declarations for the `Video` and `Customer` classes. The `Video` class grants friendship to the `Customer` class.

Example 3-10 ▶

```
// video.h
#ifndef VIDEO_H
#define VIDEO_H
class Video;  // Forward declaration
class Customer
{
  public:
    // Other method declarations for the Customer class
    int query(Video&);
```

```
      private:
        char* name;
        char* address;
        char* phone;
    };
    class Video
    {
      public:
        // Other method declarations for the Video class
        // Friendship granted to the Customer class
        friend class Customer;
      private:
        char* name;
        char* producer;
        short quantity;
    };
    #endif
```

Exercise 3.1

MODIFY

You have written a C++ appointment-scheduling program for a dentist that uses the `Date`, `Customer`, and `Time` classes. Your program is saved as Ch3-1.cpp in the Chapter3 folder on your Student Disk, and your class files are saved as time.h, date.h, customer.h, time.cpp, date.cpp, and customer.cpp. Your program accepts input in the form of a customer's name and telephone number and then stores the data in a `Customer` object. It also accepts input about an appointment by storing the appointment date (month, day, and year) in a `Date` object and the appointment time (hour and minutes) in a `Time` object. You wrote a `print()` function for each of the three classes. Modify the program and class files to use one `print()` function that is a friend of the three classes. You will need to create another .cpp file for the friend `print()` function. When you have finished, save your modified files as timea.h, datea.h, customera.h, timea.cpp, datea.cpp, customera.cpp, and Ch3-1a.cpp in the Chapter3 folder. Save any additional files you need with meaningful filenames.

Exercise 3.2 ▶

DEBUG

The course schedule program saved as Ch3-2.cpp in the Chapter3 folder on your Student Disk uses a `Section` object and an `Instructor` object. You want to grant friendship to the `Section` object's methods so that you can print the `Section` information (course number, section number, days of week, time of day, and room number) along with the `Instructor` information (name and rank). The `Section` class files are saved as section.h and section.cpp, and the `Instructor` class files are saved as instructor.h and instructor.cpp in the Chapter3 folder. The current version of your program does not compile correctly. Study the files and then fix the problems so that your program grants friendship correctly. When you have finished, save your corrected files as Ch3-2a.cpp, sectiona.h, sectiona.cpp, instructora.h, and instructora.cpp in the Chapter3 folder.

Exercise 3.3 ▶

DEVELOP

Michael Fixx, the owner of Fixx It Auto Shop, has asked you to write a C++ program that will manage information about vehicles and the mechanics who worked on them. Your program should use a friend function to print a report that includes each mechanic's name and information about each vehicle he or she services. Create an array of 10 `Vehicle` objects and a second array of five `Mechanic` objects. Populate the `Vehicle` array with the vehicle's make, model, year, and required repairs. Populate the `Mechanic` array with the mechanic's name and specialization (such as brake jobs, transmission overhaul, and so on). The mechanics' names and areas of specialization are as follows:

Name	Specialty
Sam Breakstone	Brake repair
Laura Lube	Oil change
Carlos Circle	Tire rotation
Sartha Speed	Transmission repair
Carrie Coldwater	Air-conditioning repair

After you populate the `Vehicle` and `Mechanic` objects with data, generate a report that lists the required repairs along with the mechanic who will perform the work, based on his or her listed specialty. When you have finished, save your program as Ch3-3a.cpp and your class files as auto.h, auto.cpp, mechanic.h, and mechanic.cpp in the Chapter3 folder on your Student Disk.

Inline Functions

Each time a function is called, the system transfers program control to the called function. When the called function finishes executing, program control transfers back to the calling function. This activity creates overhead for your program; that is, the time incurred by the function calls might impact your program's performance.

An **inline function** is a function whose code is substituted in your program in place of an actual call to that function. Using inline functions lets you avoid delays caused by system overhead. In the C programming language, you can write macros to avoid system overhead. Although C++ also supports macros, most programmers use inline functions because they work better with other C++ features for the following reasons:

- Inline functions may be methods; macros cannot.
- Inline functions may be friends; macros cannot.
- Inline functions may be overloaded; macros cannot.
- Inline function arguments obey parameter-passing rules; macro arguments do not.

You can write global inline functions or create inline methods for a class. Writing an inline function is usually the better option when it is small (a few lines of code) and not called from too many places from within the program. Although calling an inline function repeatedly will decrease your program's execution time, it creates one disadvantage. Use of such functions increases your program's size to a considerable extent because the system replaces the function call with the code, which increases the total number of lines of code.

To write a global inline function, you must place the function definition before the function that uses it and provide the keyword `inline` before the return data type of the function. Example 3-11 shows a C++ program that uses the inline function named `max()`.

Example 3-11 ▶

```
// Ex3-11.cpp
#include <iostream.h>
inline int max(int value1, int value2)
{
  return (value1 > value2 ? value1 : value2);
}
int main()
{
  int number1 = 50;
```

```
      int number2 = 100;
      cout << "The largest number is " << max(number1,number2)
           << '.' << endl;
      return 0;
}
```

Output:
```
The largest number is 100.
```

When you write an inline class method, you can put the code in the class declaration. In Example 3-12, the method get_name( ) has been inlined. When you include the code in the class declaration, you do not need to use the keyword inline.

Example 3-12 ▶

```
// video.h
#ifndef VIDEO_H
#define VIDEO_H
class Video
{
  public:
    // Default constructor
    Video(char* = "", char* = "", short =0);
    Video(const Video&);  // Copy constructor
    ~Video();  // Destructor
    // Overloaded operators
    int operator==(Video&);
    Video& operator=(Video&);
    short operator+(Video&);
    Video& operator++();
    Video& operator++(int);

    void set_all(char* = "", char* = "", short = 0);

    // The get_name() method has been inlined
    const char* get_name()
    {
      return name;
    }
    const char* get_producer();
    short get_quantity();
    // print() is a friend function
    friend void print(Video&);
  private:
    char* name;
    char* producer;
    short quantity;
};
#endif
```

The code style shown in Example 3-12 clutters up the class declaration. Example 3-13 shows a better style, which places the inline function's definition outside of the class declaration, but still in the header file for the class.

Example 3-13 ▶

```cpp
// video.h
#ifndef VIDEO_H
#define VIDEO_H
class Video
{
  public:
    // Default constructor
    Video(char* = "", char* = "", short = 0);
    Video(const Video&);  // Copy constructor
    ~Video();  // Destructor
    // Overloaded operators
    int operator==(Video&);
    Video& operator=(Video&);
    short operator+(Video&);
    Video& operator++();
    Video& operator++(int);

    void set_all(char* = "", char* = "", short = 0);

    const char* get_name();
    const char* get_producer();
    short get_quantity();
    // print() is a friend function
    friend void print(Video&);
  private:
    char* name;
    char* producer;
    short quantity;
};
inline const char* Video::get_name()
{
  return name;
}
#endif
```

A few problems arise when you use inline functions. One goal of object-oriented programming is to hide implementation details from the class user (the programmer) so that modifying the class does not affect programs that use it. Using inline functions violates the principle of implementation hiding because the code for methods appears in header files. With this approach, whenever the class author modifies the class, the programs that use the class must be recompiled as well. Another problem arises from the fact that the compiler does not always honor your request for an inline function. For example, if the function contains a loop, C++ will not inline the function; instead, it will generate an error or warning message at compile time. If the header file with the inlined function appears multiple times, an error message will indicate that the inline function has duplicate definitions. To solve this problem, you should put the function in a separate .cpp file and include it once at compile time; alternatively, you can precompile the function and then link it to your source code files.

Exercise 3.4 ▶

In Exercise 3.1, you used the Date, Time, and Customer classes and wrote a friend function that needed access to the private data members of all three classes. Now you will modify the three classes to use inline functions. The following files are saved in the Chapter3 folder on your Student Disk: date1.cpp, date1.h, time1.cpp, time1.h, customer1.cpp, and customer1.h. Make the appropriate modifications, being sure to inline at least two methods in each class, and then save the files as date1a.cpp, date1a.h, time1a.cpp, time1a.h, customer1a.cpp, and customer1a.h. Use the Ch3-1.cpp program to test your modified classes.

Exercise 3.5 ▶

You use a C++ program to manage your checking account. Recently, you modified the BankAccount class to take advantage of inline functions. This program will not link, so you do not know whether it works correctly. Find and fix the errors in the files named bank.h, bank.cpp, and Ch3-5.cpp. When you have finished, save the corrected files as banka.h, banka.cpp, and Ch3-5a.cpp in the Chapter3 folder on your Student Disk.

Exercise 3.6 ▶

Write a C++ program that allows you to appraise the value of your Beanie Baby collection. Write a Beanie class whose objects will store the following information: Beanie name, purchase price, current price, retired (y or n), and quantity. The Beanie Baby data are saved as beanie.dat and should be read into an array of 10 Beanie objects. Your program should calculate the total purchase amount for your collection, your collection's current value, and the difference between the purchase price and the current price. When you have finished, save your program as Ch3-6a.cpp and your class files as beanie.h and beanie.cpp in the Chapter3 folder on your Student Disk.

Constants

To declare C++ constants, you use the keyword const. You must initialize all constants, and you cannot change their values in your programs. Constants passed as arguments to functions can be passed by value, as a constant reference, or as a pointer to a constant. Constant objects can invoke only constant methods. A constant method, which sometimes is called an **accessor** or an **inspector**, can access only the value of class data members; accessors cannot change their values.

Declaring Constants

When you declare a C++ constant, you precede the variable's name and its data type with the keyword const. Example 3-14 shows the statements to declare and initialize three constants.

Example 3-14 ▶

```
const int MAX_AGE = 125;
const double PI = 3.14159;
const int SEC_IN_MINUTE = 60;
```

When using pointers in C++, you can declare the pointer as a constant, which means that you cannot change the address stored in the pointer variable, but you *can* change what it points to. The C++ code shown in Example 3-15 declares ptr as a const character pointer and initializes the pointer to point to the "Hello" string. Because ptr is a constant, you cannot change its value (an address), but you can change what it points to.

Example 3-15 ▶	```
	// Declares and initializes ptr as a constant
	// character pointer.
	char* const ptr = "Hello";
	ptr = "GoodBye"; // Error; cannot change contents of ptr
	*ptr = 'X'; // OK; changing the value ptr points to
	``

Figure 3-1 illustrates the declaration, initialization, and assignment statements shown in Example 3-15.

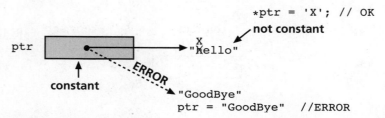

Figure 3-1: Constant pointer

You also can declare a pointer that is not a constant itself but points to a constant, meaning that you can change the value stored in the pointer (the address) but you cannot change what it points to. Example 3-16 shows this type of declaration.

Example 3-16 ▶	```
	// Declare ptr as a character pointer, initialize ptr,
	// and declare what it points to as constant.
	const char* ptr = "Hello";
	ptr = "GoodBye" // OK; changes the value of ptr
	*ptr = 'X'; // Error; cannot change what ptr points to
	``

Figure 3-2 illustrates the declaration, initialization, and assignment statements shown in Example 3-16.

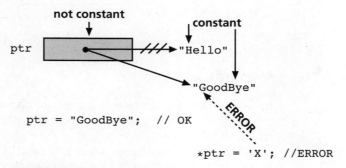

Figure 3-2: Pointer to a constant

In addition, you can declare a constant pointer to a constant, which means that you cannot change the value stored in the pointer (the address) or the value to which it points. The C++ code in Example 3-17 illustrates how to declare a constant pointer to a constant.

Example 3-17 ▶

```
// Declare ptr as a constant character pointer,
// initialize ptr, and declare what it points to as constant.

const char* const ptr = "Hello";
ptr = "GoodBye";  // Error; cannot change the value of ptr
*ptr = 'X';  // Error; cannot change what ptr points to
```

Figure 3-3 illustrates the declaration, initialization, and assignment statements shown in Example 3-17.

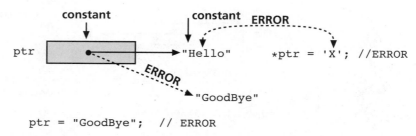

```
ptr = "GoodBye";  // ERROR
```

Figure 3-3: Constant pointer to a constant

Exercise 3.7 ▶

Evaluate each of the following C++ statements and indicate "OK" if it would compile correctly or "Error" if it would result in a compiler error.

```
int main()
{
  char* const ptr1 = "house";
  const char* ptr2 = "casa";
  const char* const ptr3 = "maison";

  ptr1 = "yes";   // _____
  *ptr1 = 'Y';    // _____
  ptr2 = "oui"    // _____
  *ptr2 = 'O';    // _____
  ptr3 = "si";    // _____
  *ptr3 = 'S';    // _____
  return 0;
}
```

Reference to a Constant

In C++, a reference can refer to a constant object only if you declare it as a reference to const. In Example 3-18, the argument passed to the change() function is a reference and the argument passed to the no_change() function is a constant reference. In the main() function, vid_item1 is a Video object and vid_item2 is a constant Video object. The argument passed to the change() function can reference vid_item1 but not vid_item2 because vid_item2 is a constant. A reference to const can refer to either a constant or a nonconstant object. Therefore, the argument passed to the no_change() function can reference either vid_item1 or vid_item2. To run the following example program, you must compile two files—Ex3-18.cpp and video.cpp—to create a single executable file.

Example 3-18 ▶

```cpp
// Ex3-18.cpp
#include "video.h"
// Might reference a Video object but not a
// const Video object.
void change(Video& video_in)
{
  Video another_object("The Apostle", "Duval Dept.", 56);
  video_in = another_object;
}
// Might reference a Video object or a const Video object
void no_change(const Video& video_in)
{
  Video another_object;
  another_object = video_in;
}
int main()
{
  // Video object
  Video vid_item1("Titanic", "Cameron Co.", 22);
  // const Video object
  const Video vid_item2("As Good As It Gets", "Jack's Inc", 43);
  no_change(vid_item1);   // OK; Video object
  no_change(vid_item2);   // OK; const Video object
  change(vid_item1);      // OK; Video object
  // Error; cannot reference a const Video object
  // change(vid_item2);
  return 0;
}
```

When you write functions with reference arguments, if the function does not need to change the value of its argument, then the argument should be a reference to const.

Pointer to a Constant

In C++, a pointer can refer to a constant object only if you declare it as a pointer to const. In Example 3-19, the argument passed to the change() function is a pointer to a Video object and the argument passed to the no_change() function is a pointer to a constant Video object. In the main() function, vid_item1 is a Video object and vid_item2 is a constant Video object. The argument passed to the change() function can point to vid_item1 but not to vid_item2 because vid_item2 is a constant. A pointer to const can point to either a constant or a nonconstant object. Therefore, the argument in the no_change() function can reference either vid_item1 or vid_item2. To run the following example program, you must compile two files—Ex3-19.cpp and video.cpp—to create a single executable file.

Example 3-19 ▶

```
// Ex3-19.cpp
#include "video.h"
// Might point to a Video object but not to a
// const Video object.
void change(Video* video_ptr)
{
  Video another_object("The Apostle", "Duval Dept.", 56);
  *video_ptr = another_object;
}
// Might point to a Video object or to a const Video object
void no_change(const Video* video_ptr)
{
  Video another_object;
  another_object = *video_ptr;
}
int main()
{
  // Video object
  Video vid_item1("Titanic", "Cameron Co.", 22);
  // const Video object
  const Video vid_item2("As Good As It Gets", "Jack's Inc",
                        43);
  no_change(&vid_item1);   // OK; Video object
  no_change(&vid_item2);   // OK; const Video object
  change(&vid_item1);      // OK; Video object
  // Error; cannot reference a const Video object
  // change(&vid_item2);
  return 0;
}
```

When you write functions with pointer arguments, if the function does not need to change the value to which its argument points, then the argument should be a pointer to const.

Passing a Constant Object by Value

You can pass constant objects by value regardless of whether the function's arguments are declared as const. When you pass arguments by value, the function receives a copy of the argument rather than the original argument, so the function cannot change the value of the actual argument.

Constant Methods

Methods belong to one of three categories: manager, implementor, or accessor. **Manager methods** perform initialization and clean-up tasks, such as constructors and destructors. **Implementor methods**, or **mutator methods**, modify the data members of a class. **Accessor methods**, or **inspector methods** or **constant methods**, return information about an object's current state without making changes. The get_name() method in the Video class is an example of an accessor function. You should write constant class methods when the method does not need to change the value of any of the private data members; this approach gives the private data additional protection from unwanted changes.

To write an accessor, you add the keyword `const` after the argument list in both the declaration and the definition. Example 3-20 shows the modified `Video` class, which includes several `const` methods and the definition for the `get_name()` method, which is now an accessor.

Example 3-20 ▶

```
// video.h
#ifndef VIDEO_H
#define VIDEO_H
class Video
{
  public:
    // Default constructor
    Video(const char* = "", const char* = "", short = 0);
    Video(const Video&);   // Copy constructor
    ~Video();              // Destructor
    // Overloaded operators
    int operator==(const Video&) const;     // Accessor
    Video& operator=(const Video&);
    short operator+(const Video&) const;    // Accessor
    Video& operator++();
    Video& operator++(int);

    void set_all(const char* = "", const char* = "", short = 0);

    const char* get_name() const;        // Accessor
    const char* get_producer() const;    // Accessor
    short get_quantity() const;          // Accessor
    // print() is a friend function
    friend void print(const Video&);
  private:
    char* name;
    char* producer;
    short quantity;
};
inline const char* Video::get_name() const
{
  return name;
}
#endif
```

To declare a constant object, you use the `const` keyword. A `const` object can invoke methods, but only if the method is a `const` method (accessor). A `const` method cannot change the data members of its invoking object, and either a `const` object or a non-`const` object can invoke it. All data members of a `const` object are also `const`, so you can initialize but not assign values to them. For this reason, when creating constant objects you must provide a constructor with an initialization list because constants may not be assigned. You learned about writing constructors with initialization lists in Chapter 2.

Exercise 3.8 ▶

Modify the `Time` class to include accessor methods when appropriate and to declare arguments to methods as `const` where appropriate. Make these modifications to the time2.h and time2.cpp files, which are saved in the Chapter3 folder on your Student Disk. Use the test program saved as Ch3-8.cpp to test your modifications but do *not* modify this program. When you have finished, save the modified files as time2a.h and time2a.cpp in the Chapter3 folder.

Exercise 3.9 ▶

You have written a `Rectangle` class and C++ program that uses it. Your program is saved as Ch3-9.cpp and your `Rectangle` class files are stored as rectangle.h and rectangle.cpp in the Chapter3 folder on your Student Disk. The `Rectangle` class provides methods for calculating the area and perimeter of a `Rectangle` object as well as drawing a `Rectangle` object. In its current state, your program does not compile. Find and fix the errors and then save the corrected files as rectanglea.h, rectanglea.cpp, and Ch3-9a.cpp in the Chapter3 folder.

Exercise 3.10 ▶

Create a `Beverage` class and a `Patron` class, and then write a C++ program that simulates a patron ordering beverages. Keep a running tab of the patron's charges. Your `Beverage` class should contain information about the type of beverage and its price. Your `Patron` class should contain the patron's name and the running total for beverages ordered. When you have finished, save your program as Ch3-10a.cpp and your class files as beveragea.h, beveragea.cpp, patrona.h, and patrona.cpp in the Chapter3 folder on your Student Disk.

Static Data Members and Methods

When you declare a static variable in C, the variable is created in the data area, initialized to a zero value, and has a lifetime that is the duration of the program. In C++, you can declare data members of a class as static, which is useful when objects of the same class must share common data. Static class data members:

- May be placed in the public or private section of a class declaration.
- Are created and initialized before the `main()` function is called.
- Are shared by all instances of the class (objects)—only one copy of the data member exists.
- May not be accessed by nonmember functions, unless they appear in the public section of the class declaration.
- Are independent of the instances of the class (objects).
- Must be initialized externally to the class declaration.

You can access a static data member in two ways. The first method is to use the name of the class, followed by the scope resolution operator, followed by the name of the static data member; Example 3-21 illustrates this approach. The static data member actually belongs to the class, so the name of the class is all that is needed.

Example 3-21 ▶

```
class_name::static_data_member_name
```

The second method is to use the name of any object of the class, followed by the dot operator, followed by the name of the static data member; Example 3-22 illustrates this approach.

Example 3-22 ▶

```
object_name.static_data_member_name
```

To declare a static data member in the class declaration, you precede the name and data type of the static data member with the keyword `static`. You also must define the static data member and provide an optional initial value for it in one of the class .cpp files. If the definition and initial value reside outside of a source file, users of the class cannot provide a different initial value without generating an error.

Example 3-23 shows the `Video` class with a static data member added, which is used to track how many videos are rented in a single day. Because all `Video` objects share this static data member, each time one of them increments the static data member, it alters the same value. Example 3-23 also shows the definition and initialization statement for the static data member.

Example 3-23 ▶

```
// video.h
#ifndef VIDEO_H
#define VIDEO_H
class Video
{
  public:
    // Default constructor
    Video(const char* = "", const char* = "", short = 0);
    Video(const Video&);   // Copy constructor
    ~Video();              // Destructor
    // Overloaded operators
    int operator==(const Video&) const;    // Accessor
    Video& operator=(const Video&);
    short operator+(const Video&) const;   // Accessor
    Video& operator++();
    Video& operator++(int);

    void set_all(const char* = "", const char* = "", short = 0);

    const char* get_name() const;       // Accessor
    const char* get_producer() const;   // Accessor
    short get_quantity() const;         // Accessor
    // print() is a friend function
    friend void print(const Video&);
  private:
    char* name;
    char* producer;
    short quantity;
    // Declaration; incremented each time a video is rented
    static int total_num;
};
#endif

// video.cpp
int Video::total_num = 0;   // Definition and initialization
// Other methods for the Video class follow
```

Class methods can be static as well. Static methods are useful when you need to access data that relate to an entire class. You can invoke static methods, like static data members, by using the name of the class or the name of any object of that class. Example 3-24 shows both techniques for invoking a static method.

Example 3-24 ▶

```
// Using the name of the class
class_name::static_method(arguments);
// Using the name of an object
object_name.static_method(arguments);
```

Like static data members, static methods also are **instance-independent**, which means that they technically do not have an invoking object and therefore do not have access to the this pointer. You cannot declare static methods as accessors using the const keyword; they are allowed only to access and manipulate static data members. In Example 3-25, a static method has been added to the Video class declaration. The static method, which is named get_total(), returns the value of the static data member, total_num. Example 3-25 also shows the function definition for get_total() and a C++ program that uses the static data member and static method. To run the following example program, you must compile two files—Ex3-25.cpp and video.cpp—to create a single executable file.

Example 3-25 ▶

```
// video.h
#ifndef VIDEO_H
#define VIDEO_H
class Video
{
  public:
    // Default constructor
    Video(const char* = "", const char* = "", short = 0);
    Video(const Video&);  // Copy constructor
    ~Video();             // Destructor
    // Overloaded operators
    int operator==(const Video&) const;    // Accessor
    Video& operator=(const Video&);
    short operator+(const Video&) const;   // Accessor
    Video& operator++();
    Video& operator++(int);

    void set_all(const char* = "", const char* = "", short = 0);

    const char* get_name() const;        // Accessor
    const char* get_producer() const;    // Accessor
    short get_quantity() const;          // Accessor
    // print() is a friend function
    friend void print(const Video&);
    // New method; increments static data member
    void rent_one();
    // Static method
    static int get_total();
  private:
    char* name;
    char* producer;
    short quantity;
    // Declaration; incremented each time a video is rented
    static int total_num;
};
#endif
```

```cpp
// video.cpp
#include "video.h"
int Video::total_num = 0;   // Definition and initialization
void Video::rent_one()
{
  total_num++;
}
// Static method; may access and manipulate
// only static data members.
int Video::get_total()
{
  return total_num;
}
// Other methods for the Video class follow

// Ex3-25.cpp
#include <iostream.h>
#include <string.h>
#include "video.h"
int main()
{
  Video vid_item1("Titanic", "Cameron Co.", 34);
  Video vid_item2("As Good As It Gets", "Jack's Inc.", 22);
  vid_item1.rent_one();
  cout << Video::get_total() << " video(s) have been rented."
      << endl;
  vid_item2.rent_one();
  cout << Video::get_total() << " video(s) have been rented."
      << endl;
  return 0;
}
```

Output:
```
1 video(s) have been rented.
2 video(s) have been rented.
```

Exercise 3.11 ▶

You have written a C++ program that tracks your bicycle outings. The Outing class lets you record where you went, the distance traveled, and a short description of the bike trail. You created an array of Outing objects and calculated the total number of miles you traveled on your bike. Now you would like to modify the Outing class to include a static data member to store the total miles you biked and a service schedule for your bike. When you bought your bike last month, the salesperson asked you to return it for free servicing after you had ridden it 200 miles. Modify the Ch3-11.cpp program and class files that are saved as outing.h and outing.cpp in the Chapter3 folder on your Student Disk. When you have finished, save the modified files as Ch3-11a.cpp, outinga.h, and outinga.cpp in the Chapter3 folder.

Exercise 3.12 ▶

You work for the Speedy Software Company. Your current assignment is to help redesign the company's Web page to incorporate many of the additional features supported by new browser versions. You have written a C++ program to track the number of overtime hours you have worked each month to meet your deadlines. Although your program is nearly complete, it still has a few bugs that keep it from linking correctly. Find and fix the errors in the Ch3-12.cpp program that is saved in the Chapter3 folder on your Student Disk. This program uses the `WorkDay` class. The `WorkDay` class files are saved as workday.h and workday.cpp in the Chapter3 folder. When you have finished, save the corrected files as Ch3-12a.cpp, workdaya.h, and workdaya.cpp in the Chapter3 folder.

Exercise 3.13 ▶

The owner of the Recently Read Used Book Store has asked you to write a C++ program to manage the total number of books sold daily. Write a `Book` class to store the title, price, ISBN number, and number sold for each book. In addition, the program should calculate the total number of books sold. It should produce a report at the end of each day with the following information printed for each book sold that day: title, price, number sold, and total sales in dollars. After printing this information, your program should display the total number of books sold and the book sales in dollars for that day. When you have finished, save your program as Ch3-13a.cpp and your class files as booka.h and booka.cpp in the Chapter3 folder on your Student Disk.

SUMMARY

- Friend functions are given access to the private data members of a class. You can grant friendship to nonmember functions, methods of another class, or another class.
- Friend functions are not invoked with an object and therefore do not have access to the `this` pointer. They must have an object passed to them as an argument.
- To declare a function as a friend, you use the keyword `friend`.
- Two or more classes may grant friendship to the same friend function.
- An inline function is a function whose code is substituted in your program in place of an actual call to that function, which reduces the system overhead incurred by function calls and can improve the run-time performance of your program. Using inline functions, however, can increase the size of your program.
- To specify an inline function, you use the keyword `inline`. You can specify global functions or class methods as inline functions.
- To declare a constant, you use the keyword `const`. You must initialize constants, and you cannot change them in your program.
- A constant can be passed to functions by value, as a constant reference, or as a pointer to a constant.
- Constant objects can invoke only constant methods.
- A constant method can access only the values of class data members. It cannot change their values.
- Constant methods are known as accessors or inspectors.
- Static data members are shared by all instances of the class because only one copy of the data member exists.
- To access static data members, you use the name of the class or a class object.
- To declare a static data member, you use the keyword `static`.
- Static data members must be defined in any of the class .cpp files. You can initialize static data members when you define them.
- Like static data members, static methods are instance-independent.
- To invoke static methods, you use the name of the class or an instance of the class.
- Because you can invoke static methods without a class object, these methods do not have access to the `this` pointer.
- Static methods are allowed only to access and manipulate static data members.

PROGRESSIVE PROJECTS

1. Green Grocery Online Shopping Program

In Chapter 2, you created all the needed constructors for the `GroceryItem` class using default function arguments, if appropriate. You also changed the implementation of the `item_name` to use dynamically allocated memory instead of an array of characters and wrote a destructor for the class. In addition, you overloaded the comparison operators.

In this chapter, you will create a second class named `Customer` that will keep track of each customer's name, address, and total bill. Write the methods for the `Customer` class, including a method named `pick_one()`. Pass a `GroceryItem` object to the `pick_one()` method so that you can add its price to the `Customer` object's total bill. The `GroceryItem` class should grant friendship to the `Customer` class. Use constants, constant methods, and inline functions where appropriate.

Simulate a customer shopping by picking items from the array of Grocery objects and then calculating a total bill.

When you have finished, save your program as Ch3-pp1.cpp and your class files as grocery.h, grocery.cpp, customer.h, and customer.cpp in the Chapter3 folder on your Student Disk.

2. Modified Five-Card Stud Poker

In Chapter 2, you created all the needed constructors for the `Card` class using default function arguments, if appropriate. You also changed the implementation of the `suit` data member to use dynamically allocated memory instead of an array of characters and added a destructor for the class. In addition, you overloaded the comparison operators to make sorting a player's hand easier.

In this chapter, you will add a new class named `Dealer` that will include the dealer's name and methods to assign a value to the `name` data member and return the `name` data member. Also, you will include a method named `deal_one()` that is passed a player's `Card` object and the deck of `Card` objects. The `deal_one()` method should generate a random number between 0 and 51 that represents the card dealt from the deck. Mark the dealt card as used, and assign the values (suit and type) to the player's `Card` object that was passed to this method. The `Card` class should grant friendship to the `Dealer` class. Use constants, constant methods, and inline functions where appropriate.

Continue to simulate a game of modified five-card stud poker by dealing five cards to four players, sorting the player's hands, and then displaying their hands. You can also ask for the dealer's name and display it before the poker game begins.

When you have finished, save your program as Ch3-pp2.cpp and your class files as card.h, card.cpp, dealer.h, and dealer.cpp in the Chapter3 folder on your Student Disk.

INDEPENDENT PROJECTS

1. Sweet Nothings Dessert Shop

Mary Moretti is the manager of the Sweet Nothings Dessert Shop. She has asked you to write a C++ program that will store information about daily dessert sales, including the number of each dessert item sold, the total number of desserts sold, and the total sales in dollars. Currently, the shop offers 10 different dessert items. Your program should read the dessert data into an array of `Dessert` objects. The data for each dessert (name and price) are saved as dessert.dat in the Chapter3 folder on your Student Disk. Use the appropriate C++ class features, including constants and constant data functions, inline functions, and static data members and static methods, as you develop this project. When you have finished, save your program as Ch3-ip1.cpp and your class files as dessert.h and dessert.cpp in the Chapter3 folder on your Student Disk.

2. Paws and Claws Clinic

Bob Beagle, the owner of the Paws and Claws Animal Clinic, has asked you to write a C++ program that will track the animal patients that visit his clinic. He wants to store the following information about each scheduled appointment: the animal's name, type (dog or cat), age, ailment, and the appointment date and time. The program should let Bob print a report that lists all scheduled appointments. It should first read in the appointment data from the file named dogs_cats.dat that is saved in the Chapter3 folder on your Student Disk. Once the data are read, it should print the report. You should use three classes in the solution to this problem: a `Patient` class, a `Vet_time` class, and a `Vet_date` class. When you have finished, save your class files as vet_time.h, vet_time.cpp, vet_date.h, vet_date.cpp, patient.h, and patient.cpp and save your program as Ch3-ip2.cpp in the Chapter3 folder.

Reusing C++ Classes

Introduction ▶ In this chapter, you will reuse existing classes after their initial implementations and examine the differences between creating classes that use a "has-a" relationship and an "is-a" relationship. In addition, you will create new classes using composition (has-a relationship) or inheritance (is-a relationship). You also will declare and define a derived class, redefine methods, write constructors for your derived classes, and use a derived class in a C++ program.

Relationships: "Has-a" Versus "Is-a"

Reusing existing code is one of the primary advantages of object-oriented programming. You can use several techniques to reuse C++ classes. The first technique, called **composition**, involves placing an object of an existing class type within a new class. You create a new class composed of members that might belong to another class. The new class now **has-a** member or members that are another class type.

The second technique, called **inheritance**, involves creating a new class based on an existing class. To use inheritance, you create a new class (called the **derived class**) that contains every member of the original class (called the **base class**). You can then modify the derived class by adding members that allow it to behave in new ways. You also can redefine methods that are inherited from the base class if they do not meet your exact needs in the derived class.

The derived class **is-a** type of base class. For example, if you create a base class named `Vehicle` and then derive a new class named `Automobile` from the base class, you can say that an `Automobile` **is-a** `Vehicle`.

Exercise 4.1 ▶   For each problem description, write on a piece of paper whether it would be better to use composition (has-a relationship) or inheritance (is-a relationship):

    a. A restaurant owner wants to maintain a list of the dinners that he serves at his establishment. A dinner includes a salad item, an entrée item, and a dessert item.

    b. The local library wants to maintain information about the following types of reference books in its collection: encyclopedia, dictionary, thesaurus, and atlas.

    c. A college bookstore wants to maintain a list of the books required for the sections of courses offered this semester. Each section includes a course number, section number, instructor name, primary text, and additional texts.

    d. You are writing a graphics program that requires you to draw and maintain information about the following shapes: circle, square, triangle, and line.

    e. You operate a small bookstore and sell various types of publications. You need to maintain information about books, magazines, and newspapers.

    f. You would like to write an appointment-scheduler program. For each appointment, you need information about the person's name and the appointment's date and time.

Using Composition

To reuse classes by taking advantage of composition, you simply create a new class and include data member(s) in the new class that are instances of another class. For example, in Chapters 1, 2, and 3 you used the `Video` class, which already is implemented. In this chapter, suppose you would like to create a new class to maintain information about every in-stock video.

Declaring a New Class That Uses Composition

The `Inventory` class takes advantage of composition by including a data member that is an array of 200 `Video` objects. When you create an instance of the `Inventory` class, you also create 200 `Video` objects; thus a `Video` class constructor will be called 200 times. Likewise, when an `Inventory` class object is destroyed, the `Video` class destructor is called 200 times. You must write constructors and a destructor for the `Inventory` class. The `Inventory` class constructors and destructor will then be used together with the `Video` class constructors and destructor when you create an `Inventory` class object. When you create the object, the `Video` constructor is invoked 200 times, followed by the invocation of the `Inventory` class constructor. To destroy the object, the `Inventory` destructor is invoked, followed by the `Video` destructor being called 200 times.

You also should write a copy constructor for the new `Inventory` class because you might want to create a new `Inventory` object from an existing `Inventory` object. When writing the copy constructor, you can rely on the `Video` class copy constructor to deal with the data members that are `Video` objects.

In addition, you might want to overload operators for the `Inventory` class. For example, you might find it useful to assign one `Inventory` object to another. In that case, you must overload the assignment operator (=). Just as you could rely on the `Video` constructor being called when you create an `Inventory` object, if the contained `Video` class has overloaded the assignment operator, then that overloaded operator will handle assignments that deal with the `Video` objects.

Example 4-1 shows the class declaration for the new `Inventory` class.

Example 4-1 ▶

```
// inventory.h
#ifndef INVENTORY_H
#define INVENTORY_H
#include "video.h" // Video class header file
const int MAX_VIDEOS = 200;
class Inventory
{
  public:
    Inventory();  // Default constructor
    Inventory(const Inventory&);  // Copy constructor
    // Assignment operator
    Inventory& operator=(const Inventory&);
    // Retrieve number of videos in array
    short get_num_videos()const;
    // Assign values to a Video object
    void set_video_info(const char*, const char*, short);
    // Print information about videos
    void print_video_info()const;

  private:
    // Inventory class "has-an" array of 200 Video objects
    Video all_videos[MAX_VIDEOS];
    short num_videos;
};
#endif
```

Notice that you must include the header file that contains the class declaration for the `Video` class to ensure that the compiler knows about the `Video` class before you declare a data member in the `Inventory` class of the `Video` class type. An additional data member, `num_videos`, has been added to the `Inventory` class as well as a method, `get_num_videos()`, that retrieves the value of the new data member. Other methods used to assign and retrieve information stored in the array of `Video` objects also are included in the `Inventory` class. The new data member `num_videos` holds the actual number of videos that are stored in the `all_videos` array. The maximum size of this array is `MAX_VIDEOS` (or 200), though some of the 200 elements of the array might not contain valid data. The data member `num_videos` holds the number of valid `Video` objects currently in the inventory.

Exercise 4.2 ▶

The following C++ code declares a `Time` class. Use the `Time` class to create a new class named `OS_job`, which represents jobs submitted to a computer operating system for processing. Your new class should contain the following information: job number, priority (ranging from 1 to 10), and a time stamp that indicates when the job was submitted (hour, minute, and second). Write your `OS_job` class declaration on a piece of paper.

```cpp
// time.h
#ifndef TIME_H
#define TIME_H
class Time
{
  public:
    // Constructor
    Time(int = 0, int = 0, int = 0);
    Time(const Time&);  // Copy constructor
    // Overloaded assignment operator
    Time& operator=(const Time&);
    // Assign values to data members
    void set_values(int = 0, int = 0, int = 0);
    void set_hour(int = 0);
    void set_minute(int = 0);
    void set_second(int = 0);
    // Retrieve values from data members
    int get_hour()const;
    int get_minute()const;
    int get_second()const;
    void print()const;  // Print values of data members
  private: // Data members
    int hour;
    int minute;
    int second;
};
#endif
```

Defining a Class That Uses Composition

After writing the `Inventory` class declaration, you must implement its methods. Example 4-2 shows the method definitions.

Example 4-2 ▶

```cpp
// inventory.cpp
#include "inventory.h"
#include <iostream.h>
Inventory::Inventory()  // Default constructor
{
  int k;
  // Initialize all Video objects with 0 values
  for(k = 0; k < MAX_VIDEOS; k++)
    // Uses Video set_all() method
    all_videos[k].set_all("","",0);
```

```
    num_videos = 0;
}
// Copy constructor
Inventory::Inventory(const Inventory& inventory_in)
{
  int k;
  for(k = 0; k < inventory_in.num_videos; k++)
    // Uses the Video class assignment operator
    all_videos[k] = inventory_in.all_videos[k];
  num_videos = inventory_in.num_videos;
}
// Overloaded assignment operator
Inventory& Inventory::operator=(const Inventory& inventory_in)
{
  int k;
  for(k = 0; k < inventory_in.num_videos; k++)
    // Uses the Video class assignment operator
    all_videos[k] = inventory_in.all_videos[k];
  num_videos = inventory_in.num_videos;
  return *this;
}
short Inventory::get_num_videos()const
{
  return num_videos;
}
void Inventory::set_video_info(const char* name_in,
  const char* producer_in, short qty_in)
{
  // Uses Video class set_all() method
  all_videos[num_videos].set_all(name_in, producer_in, qty_in);
  num_videos++;   // Tracks number of valid Videos
}
void Inventory::print_video_info()const
{
  int k;
  for(k = 0; k < num_videos; k++)
  {
    // Use Video methods
    cout << "Name:  " << all_videos[k].get_name() << endl;
    cout << "Producer:  " << all_videos[k].get_producer()
         << endl;
    cout << "Quantity:  " << all_videos[k].get_quantity()
         << endl;
  }
}
```

Exercise 4.3 ▶ You wrote the OS_job class declaration in Exercise 4.2. Now, on a piece of paper, write the method definitions for the OS_job class.

Using the Inventory Class in a C++ Program

Now you are ready to use the new Inventory class in a C++ program. Example 4-3 illustrates how to create an Inventory object, how to assign data to several Video class objects contained within the Inventory class object, and how to retrieve data about the videos from the Inventory object. To run the following example program, you must compile three files—inventory.ccp, video.ccp, and Ex4-3.ccp—to create a single executable file.

Example 4-3 ▶

```cpp
// Ex4-3.cpp
#include "inventory.h"
int main()
{
  // Inventory constructor invoked after
  // the Video constructor is called 200 times.
  Inventory  family_videos;
  // Create a second Inventory object
  Inventory copy2;
  // Add information about a Video to the inventory
  family_videos.set_video_info("Titanic","Cameron Co.",56);
  // Add information about a Video to the inventory
  family_videos.set_video_info("As Good As It Gets",
    "Jack's, Inc.", 20);
  // Use the copy constructor
  Inventory copy = family_videos;
  // Use overloaded assignment operator
  copy2 = copy;
  // Print data about Videos in the inventory
  family_videos.print_video_info();
  // Use copy to print data about Videos in the inventory
  copy.print_video_info();
  // Use another copy to print data
  // about Videos in the inventory.
  copy2.print_video_info();
  return 0;
}
```

Output:

```
Name:  Titanic
Producer:  Cameron Co.
Quantity:  56
Name:  As Good As It Gets
Producer:  Jack's, Inc.
Quantity:  20
Name:  Titanic
Producer:  Cameron Co.
Quantity:  56
Name:  As Good As It Gets
Producer:  Jack's, Inc.
Quantity:  20
Name:  Titanic
Producer:  Cameron Co.
```

```
Quantity:  56
Name:  As Good As It Gets
Producer:  Jack's, Inc.
Quantity:  20
```

Exercise 4.4 ▶

The See Clearly Optical Supply Company uses a C++ program to maintain information about the eyeglasses it supplies to various distributors of optical devices. The current version of the program uses an array of `Eyeglass` objects to store information about the products. Modify the C++ program saved as Ch4-4.cpp in the Chapter4 folder on your Student Disk by creating an `Inventory` class that has two members: an array of `Eyeglass` objects and the number of `Eyeglass` objects in the array that now store valid data. Save the modified program as Ch4-4a.cpp and save your new class files as glass_inv.h and glass_inv.cpp in the Chapter4 folder. Use the data file named eyeglass.dat to test your new program. The `Eyeglass` class files are saved as eyeglass.h and eyeglass.ccp in the Chapter4 folder.

Exercise 4.5 ▶

You have written a C++ program for a local restaurant that maintains a list of items on its dinner menu. The program works with a new class you created named the `Dinners` class. The `Dinners` class files are saved as dinners.h and dinners.cpp and your program is saved as Ch4-5.cpp in the Chapter4 folder on your Student Disk. Your program should read in the dinner-menu information from a file named dinners.dat and then print the information in an attractive format. Because your program does not compile, however, you do not know whether it produces the correct results. Find and fix the errors. Save the corrected program as Ex4-5a.cpp and the `Dinners` class files as dinnersa.h and dinnersa.cpp in the Chapter4 folder. A dinner is made up of an `Entree`, a `Salad`, and a `Dessert` object. The class files for these objects are saved as salad.h, salad.ccp, entree.h, entree.ccp, dessert.h, and dessert.ccp in the Chapter4 folder.

Exercise 4.6 ▶

Use the `OS_job` class you created in Exercises 4.2 and 4.3 to develop a C++ program that simulates an operating system by assigning a job number, priority, and time stamp to jobs arriving for processing by the CPU (central processing unit). Job numbers, priorities, and time stamp data for 10 OS jobs are saved in the file named job_info.dat in the Chapter4 folder on your Student Disk. A single space separates each value (`job_no job_priority hour minute second`) in the job_info.dat file. For example, the value 4 10 11 33 03 represents job number 4, priority 10, received at 11:33:03.

Read in the data from the input file and then print a job listing in a format of your choice. Save your program as Ch4-6a.cpp and save your class files as OS_job.h and OS_job.cpp in the Chapter4 folder.

Using Inheritance

To reuse classes by taking advantage of inheritance, you create a new class by inheriting the members of an existing class, adding more data members and methods, and possibly by overriding or rewriting inherited methods. Any class can serve as a base class in C++. For example, a video rental store's inventory consists of videotapes and video recorders. You have implemented an `Inventory_base` class that contains the quantity, price, and description of an inventory item; methods that retrieve the values of the data items stored in the `Inventory_base` class and methods that assign values to the data members; and constructors and a destructor for the `Inventory_base` class. Example 4-4 shows the class declaration for the `Inventory_base` class.

Example 4-4 ▶

```
// inventory_base.h
#ifndef INVENTORY_BASE_H
#define INVENTORY_BASE_H
class Inventory_base
{
  public:
    // Constructor
    Inventory_base(const char* = "", short = 0,
      double = 0.0);
    // Copy constructor
    Inventory_base(const Inventory_base&);
    ~Inventory_base();  // Destructor
    // Assign values to data members
    void set_values(const char*, short, double);
    void print() const; // Print values of data members
    // Return description data member
    const char* get_description() const;
    short get_quantity() const;  // Return quantity data member
    double get_price() const;    // Return price data member
  private: // Data members
    char* description;
    short quantity;
    double price;
};
#endif
```

Example 4-5 shows the method definitions for the `Inventory_base` class.

Example 4-5 ▶

```
// inventory_base.cpp
#include <iostream.h>
#include <string.h>
#include "inventory_base.h"
// Constructor
Inventory_base::Inventory_base(const char* desc_in,
  short qty_in, double price_in):
  quantity(qty_in), price(price_in)  // Initialization list
{
  description = new char[strlen(desc_in) + 1];
  strcpy(description, desc_in);
}
// Copy constructor
Inventory_base::Inventory_base(const Inventory_base&
  inventory_in)
{
  description = new char[strlen(inventory_in.description) + 1];
  strcpy(description, inventory_in.description);
  quantity = inventory_in.quantity;
  price = inventory_in.price;
}
```

```
// Destructor
Inventory_base::~Inventory_base()
{
  delete [] description;
}
// Assigns values to data members
void Inventory_base::set_values(const char* desc_in,
  short qty_in, double price_in)
{
  delete [] description;
  description = new char[strlen(desc_in) + 1];
  strcpy(description, desc_in);
  quantity = qty_in;
  price = price_in;
}
// Prints values of data members
void Inventory_base::print() const
{
  cout << "Description:  " << description << endl;
  cout << "Quantity:  " << quantity << endl;
  cout << "Price:  $" << price << endl;
}
// Returns value of description data member
const char* Inventory_base::get_description()const
{
  return description;
}
// Returns value of quantity data member
short Inventory_base::get_quantity() const
{
  return quantity;
}
// Returns value of price data member
double Inventory_base::get_price() const
{
  return price;
}
```

The `Inventory_base` class is already implemented; now you can take advantage of inheritance to create two new classes named `Video_tape` and `Video_machine`. Both of the new classes can inherit the common attributes of the `Inventory_base` class. Because a videotape is not exactly the same as a video recorder, however, you must add data members and methods to the new classes and rewrite inherited methods. For example, you will want to include data about a video's producer for the `Video_tape` class and data about the video's manufacturer for the `Video_machine` class. You also might want to rewrite the `print()` method that was inherited from the `Inventory_base` class.

In Example 4-5, the `Inventory_base` class contains the common members and is called the base class. The `Video_tape` and `Video_machine` classes are derived from the base class and are called derived classes. The derived classes inherit all of the public members from the base class. They cannot access the private data members of the base class (`description`, `quantity`, and `price`) directly, but do have access to the private data members of the base class through the inherited methods.

Declaring a Derived Class

Syntax ▶

class derived_class: public base_class

In writing the declaration for a derived class, you give the derived class a name, follow it with a colon, and then specify the type of derivation you want to use. In this chapter, you will use `public` derivations, so you will use the keyword `public` after the colon. (You will learn about additional derivation types in Chapter 5.) After the derivation type, you name the base class from which you are deriving the new class.

The `public` derivation means that all of the public members of the base class will be public in the derived class. Therefore, you do not have to repeat these members in the derived class; you simply add new members or override inherited members in the declaration of the derived class. Example 4-6 shows the class declaration for the derived class `Video_tape`, and Example 4-7 shows the class declaration for the derived class `Video_machine`.

Example 4-6 ▶

```
// video_tape.h
#ifndef VIDEO_TAPE_H
#define VIDEO_TAPE_H
#include "inventory_base.h" // Base class header file
class Video_tape: public Inventory_base
{
  public:
    // Constructor
    Video_tape(const char* = "", const char* = "",
      short = 0, double = 0.0);
    Video_tape(const Video_tape&);  // Copy constructor
    ~Video_tape();  // Destructor
    void print()const;  // Override inherited print() method
    // Return value of producer data member
    const char* get_producer() const;
    // New set_values() method
    void set_values(const char* = "", const char* = "",
      short = 0, double = 0.0);
  private:
    char* producer;  // New data member
};
#endif
```

Example 4-7 ▶

```
// video_machine.h
#ifndef VIDEO_MACHINE_H
#define VIDEO_MACHINE_H
#include "inventory_base.h"  // Base class header file
class Video_machine: public Inventory_base
{
  public:
    // Constructor
    Video_machine(const char* = "", const char* = "",
      short = 0, double = 0.0);
    Video_machine(const Video_machine&);  // Copy constructor
```

```
      ~Video_machine();  // Destructor
      void print() const;  // Override inherited print() method
      // Retrieve value of manufacturer data member
      const char* get_manufacturer() const;
      // New set_values() method
      void set_values(const char* = "", const char* = "",
        short = 0, double = 0.0);
   private:
      char* manufacturer;  // New data member
};
#endif
```

Exercise 4.7 ▶ Use the following `Employee` class declaration to derive two new classes—the `Doctor` class and the `Staff` class—for a hospital application. In addition to the data stored in the `Employee` class, the `Doctor` class should contain the doctor's specialty (such as internist, pediatrician, allergist, and so on) and the number of years that the doctor has been a member of the hospital staff. The `Staff` class should contain the department name in which the staff member works and the person's job title. The `Employee` class files are saved as employee.h and employee.cpp in the Chapter4 folder on your Student Disk. Write your new class declarations on a piece of paper.

```
// employee.h
#ifndef EMPLOYEE_H
#define EMPLOYEE_H
class Employee
{
  public:
    // Constructor
    Employee(const char* = "", const char* = "",
      const char* = "", double = 0.0);
    Employee(const Employee&);  // Copy constructor
    ~Employee();  // Destructor
    // Overloaded assignment
    Employee& operator=(const Employee&);

    // Assign values to data members
    void set_values(const char* = "", const char* = "",
      const char* = "", double = 0.0);
    void print() const;  // Print values of data members
    const char* get_name() const;  // Retrieve name data member
    // Retrieve address data member
    const char* get_address() const;
    // Retrieve telephone data member
    const char* get_telephone() const;
    double get_salary() const;  // Retrieve salary data member
  private:
    char* name;
    char* address;
    char* telephone;
    double salary;
};
#endif
```

Defining a Derived Class

After writing the class declarations for the derived classes, you must write the methods. You add a constructor and a destructor to the `Video_tape` class and the `Video_machine` class. You also add a `print()` method to both derived classes. This method has a signature that is identical to the `print()` method in the base class and is rewritten in the derived class. In addition, you must rewrite the `set_values()` method in the derived classes so that you can assign values to the `producer` or `manufacturer` data member; you will then use the `set_values()` method from the base class to assign values to the data members that were inherited from the base class. The `Video_tape` class also includes a method named `get_producer()`, and the `Video_machine` class includes a method named `get_manufacturer()`. Example 4-8 shows the `get_producer()` and `get_manufacturer()` methods for the `Video_tape` and `Video_machine` classes.

Example 4-8 ▶

```
// video_tape.cpp
#include "video_tape.h"
const char* Video_tape::get_producer() const
{
   return producer;
}


// video_machine.cpp
#include "video_machine.h"
const char* Video_tape::get_manufacturer() const
{
   return manufacturer;
}
```

Exercise 4.8 ▶ On a piece of paper, write method definitions for the `Doctor` class that you created in Exercise 4.7 so you can retrieve the doctor's specialty and number of years on staff at the hospital. In addition, write method definitions for your `Staff` class so you can retrieve the department in which the staff member works and each person's job title.

Redefining Methods in a Derived Class

When you declare a method in a derived class declaration with the same signature as a method in the base class, the derived class method will override the inherited method; hence you must rewrite it for the derived class. For the example, the `print()` method needs to be rewritten because it has the same signature as the base class `print()` method. A method rewritten in this way will override the base class method so that, when the method is invoked with a derived class object, the rewritten method—not the base class method—is used. Example 4-9 shows the `print()` method added to the `Video_tape` class and the `Video_machine` class.

Example 4-9 ▶

```
// video_tape.cpp
#include "video_tape.h"
#include <iostream.h>
// Print values of data members
```

```
void Video_tape::print()const
{
  cout << "Producer:   " << producer << endl;
  // Invoke the base class print() method
  Inventory_base::print();
}
const char* Video_tape::get_producer()const
{
  return producer;
}


// video_machine.cpp
#include "video_machine.h"
#include <iostream.h>
// Print values of data members
void Video_machine::print() const
{
  cout << "Manufacturer:   " << manufacturer << endl;
  // Invoke the base class print() method
  Inventory_base::print()const;
}
const char* Video_machine::get_manufacturer() const
{
  return manufacturer;
}
```

In the `Video_tape` class, the `print()` method first prints the producer's name and then invokes the `Inventory_base` class's `print()` method to print the description, quantity, and price. In the `Video_machine` class, the `print()` method first prints the manufacturer's name and then invokes the `Inventory_base` class's `print()` method to print the description, quantity, and price. In both cases, you invoke the `Inventory_base` class's `print()` method by specifying the class name and the scope resolution operator before the name of the method.

Unlike the `print()` method, the `set_values()` methods in the `Video_tape` and `Video_machine` classes do not have the same signature as the `set_values()` method in the base class. You will rewrite the `set_values()` method in the base class for the two derived classes so that the producer (`Video_tape` class) and the manufacturer (`Video_machine` class) are assigned values and then the `Inventory` class's `set_values()` method is invoked to assign values to the `description`, `quantity`, and `price` data members. Example 4-10 shows the `set_values()` method definitions for the `Video_tape` and `Video_machine` classes.

Example 4-10 ▶

```
// video_tape.cpp
#include "video_tape.h"
// New set_values() method; assigns values to data members
void Video_tape::set_values(const char* prod_in,
  const char* desc_in, short qty_in,
  double price_in)
{
  delete [] producer;
  producer = new char[strlen(prod_in) + 1];
  strcpy(producer, prod_in);
```

```
    // Invoke base class set_values() method
    Inventory_base::set_values(desc_in, qty_in, price_in);
}
void Video_tape::print()const
{
    cout << "Producer:   " << producer << endl;
    Inventory_base::print();  // Call base class print() method
}
const char* Video_tape::get_producer()const
{
    return producer;
}

// video_machine.cpp
#include "video_machine.h"
// New set_values() method
void Video_machine::set_values(const char* manf_in,
    const char* desc_in, short qty_in,
    double price_in)
{
    delete [] manufacturer;
    manufacturer = new char[strlen(manf_in) + 1];
    strcpy(manufacturer, manf_in);
    // Invoke base class set_values() method
    Inventory_base::set_values(desc_in, qty_in, price_in);
}
void Video_machine::print()const
{
    cout << "Manufacturer:   " << manufacturer << endl;
    // Call base class print() method
    Inventory_base::print();
}
const char* Video_machine::get_manufacturer() const
{
    return manufacturer;
}
```

Overriding a base class method creates polymorphic methods—one of the advantages of object-oriented programming. In Chapter 2, you worked with polymorphism by creating multiple functions with the same name. Now, by using polymorphism with inheritance and overriding base class methods, you can invoke methods with the same name; depending on the invoking object, different methods will execute.

Exercise 4.9 ▶ On a piece of paper, add method definitions for the Doctor class that you wrote in Exercises 4.7 and 4.8 that will allow you to print and set the values of this class's data members. Add method definitions for the Staff class that will allow you to print and set the values of its data members.

Writing Constructors and a Destructor for a Derived Class

Some members of a base class are never inherited: friend functions, static data members, static methods, overloaded assignment (=) operators, constructors, and destructors. Because constructors and destructors are never inherited, you must therefore write new constructors and destructors for derived classes. A derived class constructor and a base class constructor will be invoked when you create a derived class object. The program calls the base class constructor first, followed by the derived class constructor.

The derived class is responsible for constructing the base class; thus, if the base class constructor requires arguments, then the derived class constructor must invoke a base class constructor and supply the arguments by using initialization lists. The derived class constructor determines which base class constructor and which derived class constructor to call. If a base class constructor does not need a constructor or requires only a default constructor, you do not need to supply arguments or invoke the base class constructor—it will be invoked automatically. You need only invoke a base class constructor and supply it with arguments if no default constructor exists for the class. Sometimes the derived class might not need a constructor because the default constructor will suffice, but the base class constructor requires arguments. In this case, you must write a constructor for the derived class to enable the derived class to construct its base class.

To destroy a derived class object, the program calls the derived class destructor first, followed by the base class destructor. The derived class does not have to do anything special to invoke the base class destructor; it is called automatically.

Example 4-11 shows the `Video_tape` class and the `Video_machine` class with constructors and destructors added.

Example 4-11 ▶

```cpp
// video_tape.cpp
#include <iostream.h>
#include <string.h>
#include "video_tape.h"
// Constructor
Video_tape::Video_tape(const char* prod_in, const char* desc_in,
  short qty_in, double price_in):
  // Calls base class constructor
  Inventory_base(desc_in, qty_in, price_in)
{
  producer = new char[strlen(prod_in) + 1];
  strcpy(producer, prod_in);
}
// Copy constructor
Video_tape::Video_tape(const Video_tape& video_in):
  // Calls base class copy constructor
  Inventory_base(video_in)
{
  producer = new char[strlen(video_in.producer) + 1];
  strcpy(producer, video_in.producer);
}
// Destructor
Video_tape::~Video_tape()
{
  delete [] producer;
}
// New set_values() method; assigns values to data members
void Video_tape::set_values(const char* prod_in,
  const char* desc_in, short qty_in,
  double price_in)
{
```

```cpp
      delete [] producer;
      producer = new char[strlen(prod_in) + 1];
      strcpy(producer, prod_in);
      // Calls base class set_values() method
      Inventory_base::set_values(desc_in, qty_in, price_in);
}
// Prints values of data members
void Video_tape::print()const
{
   cout << "Producer:   " << producer << endl;
   // Calls base class print() method
   Inventory_base::print();
}
const char* Video_tape::get_producer() const
{
   return producer;
}


// video_machine.cpp
#include <iostream.h>
#include <string.h>
#include "video_machine.h"
// Constructor
Video_machine::Video_machine(const char* manf_in,
   const char* desc_in, short qty_in,
   double price_in):
   // Calls base class constructor
   Inventory_base(desc_in, qty_in, price_in)
{
   manufacturer = new char[strlen(manf_in) + 1];
   strcpy(manufacturer, manf_in);
}
// Copy constructor
Video_machine::Video_machine(const Video_machine& video_in):
   // Calls base class copy constructor
   Inventory_base(video_in)
{
   manufacturer = new char[strlen(video_in.manufacturer) + 1];
   strcpy(manufacturer, video_in.manufacturer);
}
// Destructor
Video_machine::~Video_machine()
{
   delete [] manufacturer;
}
// New set_values() method; assigns values to data members
void Video_machine::set_values(const char* manf_in,
   const char* desc_in, short qty_in, double price_in)
{
   delete [] manufacturer;
   manufacturer = new char[strlen(manf_in) + 1];
   strcpy(manufacturer, manf_in);
   // Calls base class set_values() method
   Inventory_base::set_values(desc_in, qty_in, price_in);
}
```

```
// Prints values of data members
void Video_machine::print()const
{
  cout << "Manufacturer:  " << manufacturer << endl;
  // Calls base class print() method
  Inventory_base::print();
}
const char* Video_machine::get_manufacturer()const
{
  return manufacturer;
}
```

In Example 4-11, the constructor for the derived class `Video_tape` receives four arguments. It uses the first argument, `prod_in`, to assign a value to the `producer` data member. Then it invokes the `Inventory_base` class constructor, which expects three arguments: the description, quantity, and price. The constructor for the derived class `Video_machine` receives four arguments. It uses the first argument, `manf_in`, to assign a value to the `manufacturer` data member. Like the `Video_tape` class constructor, the `Video_machine` class constructor then invokes the `Inventory_base` class constructor, which expects three arguments: the description, quantity, and price.

On a piece of paper, write constructors and a destructor for the `Doctor` and `Staff` classes that you used in Exercises 4.7, 4.8, and 4.9.

Using Derived Classes in a C++ Program

Exercise 4.10 ▶

Now that you have created the derived classes `Video_tape` and `Video_machine`, you can use them in a C++ program. The C++ program shown in Example 4-12 creates a `Video_tape` object and a `Video_machine` object, and then uses inherited methods and methods that have been added to the derived classes. To run the following example program, you must compile four files—Ex4-12.ccp, inventory_base.ccp, video_machine.ccp, and video_tape.ccp—to create a single executable file.

Example 4-12 ▶

```
// Ex4-12.cpp
#include "video_tape.h"
#include "video_machine.h"
#include <iostream.h>
int main()
{
  // Invokes the base class constructor and
  // the derived class constructor.
  Video_tape rental_tape1("Cameron Co.", "Titanic", 35, 24.95);
  // Invokes the base class constructor and
  // the derived class constructor.
  Video_machine rental_machine1("Panasonic", "recorder",
    3, 324.99);
  // Invokes the default constructor
  Video_tape rental_tape2;
  // Invokes derived class copy constructor
  Video_machine rental_machine2 = rental_machine1;
```

```cpp
// Invokes the derived class set_values() method
rental_tape2.set_values("Spielberg Inc.",
  "Saving Private Ryan", 30, 29.99);
// Invokes the derived class (Video_tape) print() method
rental_tape1.print();
// Invokes the derived class (Video_machine)
// print() method.
rental_machine1.print();
// Using inherited functions
cout << "Description: " << rental_tape2.get_description()
    << endl;
cout << "Quantity:  " << rental_tape2.get_quantity() << endl;
cout << "Description:  " << rental_machine2.get_description()
    << endl;
cout << "Quantity:  " << rental_machine2.get_quantity()
    << endl;
return 0;
}
```

Output:

```
Producer:  Cameron Co.
Description:  Titanic
Quantity:  35
Price:  $24.95
Manufacturer:  Panasonic
Description:  recorder
Quantity:  3
Price:  $324.99
Description: Saving Private Ryan
Quantity:  30
Description:  recorder
Quantity:  3
```

Exercise 4.11

Bernie Threadstone, the owner of Thread's Men Store, has asked you to modify a C++ program that allows him to keep track of the men's clothing items sold in his store. The current version of the program uses a `Trouser` class and a `Shirt` class, both of which are derived from the `Clothing` class. Bernie now wants to add sweaters to the items sold in his store. Modify the C++ program so it also can process sweater information. You will need to keep track of the sweater size, its country of origin, description, and price. The current C++ program is saved as Ch4-11.cpp and the class files are saved as clothing.h, clothing.cpp, trouser.h, trouser.cpp, shirt.h, and shirt.cpp in the Chapter4 folder on your Student Disk. Save the modified program as Ch4-11a.cpp and give meaningful names to any additional class files you create. Use the data stored in the file clothing.dat to test your program.

Exercise 4.12 ▶

You are working on a C++ program for the Popular Pubs Bookstore. The bookstore sells books, magazines, and newspapers. You created a `Publications` class and derived three classes from it: `Book`, `Magazine`, and `Newspaper`. Your program reads in data from the file named pubs.dat and uses these data to populate three arrays that store `Book`, `Magazine`, or `Newspaper` objects. After reading in the data, your program creates a report listing all of the books, magazines, and newspapers currently sold by Popular Pubs. This program does not compile, however. The program is saved as Ch4-12.cpp and the class files used by the program are named publication.h, publication.cpp, book.h, book.cpp, newspaper.h, newspaper.cpp, magazine.h, and magazine.cpp; all of these files are saved in the Chapter4 folder on your Student Disk. Find and fix the errors. Save the corrected files as Ch4-12a.cpp, publicationa.h, publicationa.cpp, booksa.h, booksa.cpp, newspapera.h, and newspapera.cpp, magazinea.h, and magazinea.cpp.

Exercise 4.13 ▶

Write a C++ program that uses the Doctor and Staff classes that you used in Exercises 4.7 through 4.10. Your program should read in data stored in the files named doctor.dat and staff.dat in the Chapter4 folder on your Student Disk. Store the doctor.dat data in an array of Doctor objects and the staff.dat data in an array of Staff objects. After reading the data into the two arrays, print the names of all doctors in alphabetical order by last name along with each doctor's salary and field of specialization. Next, print the names of all staff members in alphabetical order by last name along with each person's salary and job title. Save your program as Ex4-13a.cpp and your class files as employee.h, employee.cpp, doctor.h, doctor.cpp, staff.h, and staff.cpp in the Chapter4 folder.

SUMMARY

- Reusing existing code is one advantage of object-oriented programming.
- The composition technique of reusing classes involves creating a new class that is composed of members that belong to another class.
- Composition creates classes that have a "has-a" relationship because the new class "has a" member or members that are another class type.
- Inheritance is another technique of reusing existing classes in which you create a new class based on an existing class. The existing class is called the base class, and the new class is called the derived class. The derived class contains all members of the original class.
- You can add members to a derived class. Likewise, you can rewrite or modify inherited members in the derived class.
- When a class is derived using a public derivation, all public members of the base class are public members in the derived class.
- Constructors and destructors are never inherited. Likewise, friend functions, static data members, static methods, and overloaded assignment (=) operators are never inherited.
- The derived class is responsible for constructing its base class if the base class constructor requires arguments. The derived class constructor invokes a base class constructor to accomplish this task.

PROGRESSIVE PROJECTS

1. Green Grocery Online Shopping Program

In Chapter 3, you created a second class, the Customer class, and used it to keep track of a customer's name and address and the total bill. You wrote methods for the Customer class, including one named pick_one() that allowed you to maintain a Customer object's total bill. You used friend functions, constants and constant methods, and inline functions where appropriate. Finally, you simulated a customer shopping by picking items from the array of GroceryItem objects and calculating a total bill.

In this chapter, you will create a new `Inventory` class, which will contain two data members—an array of valid `GroceryItem` objects and a `num_items` data member. The `num_items` data member stores the number of valid `GroceryItem` objects held in the array. You should write constructors and a destructor for the `Inventory` class, and you should overload the assignment operator. In addition, you should write the following methods:

- `set_item()`, to assign values to the next `GroceryItem` object in the array
- `get_num_items()`, to return the number of valid `GroceryItem` objects in the array
- `print_items()`, to print the names and prices of the `GroceryItem` objects
- `buy()`, to adjust the quantity ordered by a customer
- `display_items()`, to display the names, quantities, and a total for each `GroceryItem` selected by a customer
- `get_item()`, to return a `GroceryItem` object
- `sort()`, to sort the `GroceryItem` objects alphabetically by name

Modify your existing program and classes as necessary. Save your modified program as Ch4-pp1.cpp and your class files as grocery.h, grocery.cpp, customer.h, customer.cpp, inventory.h, and inventory.cpp in the Chapter4 folder on your Student Disk.

2. Modified Five-Card Stud Poker

In Chapter 3, you added a `Dealer` class to your project. The `Dealer` class included a method named `deal_one()` that was passed a player's `Card` object and the deck of `Card` objects. The `deal_one()` method generated a random number between 0 and 51 that represented which card from the deck was dealt. You marked the dealt card as used and then assigned the values (suit and type) to the player's `Card` object that was passed to this method. Where appropriate, you used friend functions, constants and constant methods, and inline functions. Finally, you simulated a game of modified five-card stud poker by dealing five cards to four players and displaying the players' hands.

In this chapter, you will reuse existing classes by creating a `Player` class and modifying the `Dealer` class. The `Player` class should contain the following data members: the player's `name` and an array of five `Card` objects. The `Player` class should also contain constructors, a destructor, and the following methods:

- `set_name()`, to assign a value to the `name` data member
- `get_name()`, to retrieve the value of the `name` data member
- `set_card()`, to assign values to one of the `Card` objects
- `display_hand()`, to display the values of the five `Card` objects

You will need to modify the `Dealer` class so that it contains the following data members: `name` and `deck`—an array of 52 `Card` objects.

Modify your existing program and classes as necessary. Save your modified program as Ch4-pp2.cpp and your class files as player.h, player.cpp, dealer.h, and dealer.cpp, card.h, and card.cpp in the Chapter4 folder on your Student Disk.

INDEPENDENT PROJECTS

1. Johnson C & E Construction Company

The Johnson C & E Construction Company is managing a large construction project that will require the use of three types of construction workers: millwrights, iron workers, and operating engineers. Johnson C & E has hired you to write a C++ program that will allow the company to maintain the following information about each construction worker hired for the job: name, address, telephone number, union affiliation, pay rate, hours worked, and job description.

Information regarding the three types of information for the construction worker types appears in Figure 4-1.

Millwrights	
Union: United Brotherhood of Carpenters	
Job Description	**Pay Rate**
Superintendent	$29.95
General Foreman	$28.95
Foreman	$27.95
Journeyman	$26.95
Apprentice	$21.56
Iron Workers	
Union: International Association of Bridge, Structural, and Ornamental Iron Workers	
Job Description	**Pay Rate**
Superintendent	$29.68
General Foreman	$28.68
Foreman	$27.68
Journeyman	$26.33
Operating Engineers	
Union: International Union of Operating Engineers	
Job Description	**Pay Rate**
Superintendent	$31.90
General Foreman	$30.90
Foreman	$29.90
Journeyman	$28.90
Apprentice	$27.10

Figure 4-1

Operating Engineer personnel also have a Class Number associated with each of the above job descriptions. These potential Class Numbers are 1, 2, 3, and 4; for example, an Operating Engineer Apprentice may have a Class Number of 3 or an Operating Engineer Foreman may have a Class Number of 1. Millwrights have a union local number that must be associated with each millwright. Iron workers have the name of a business agent that must be associated with each iron worker.

Write a C++ program that reads in data from the file named construction.dat and then populates three arrays with those data. The three arrays should store the information about millwrights, iron workers, and operating engineers. Your program should then print the data, first listing iron workers, then millwrights, and finally operating engineers. Use inheritance in the solution to this project.

Save your program as Ch4-ip1.cpp and your class files as worker.h worker.cpp, millwright.h, millwright.cpp, ironworker.h, ironworker.cpp, engineer.h, and engineer.cpp in the Chapter4 folder on your Student Disk.

2. Computer Parts

Write C++ classes and a C++ program that will allow you to assemble and price a computer from a computer parts list that includes the following items: processor, memory, hard drive, CD-ROM, floppy disk drive, keyboard, monitor, and mouse. Start with a `Part` class and then use inheritance to create classes for the various types of parts. Your C++ program should allow you to choose from a listing of parts and then print the desired configuration of the computer along with its total price. The data for this project are saved as computer.dat in the Chapter4 folder on your Student Disk. In your program, store these data in separate arrays of objects. You will need an array for `Processor` objects, another array for `Memory` objects, and so on. Save your class files as part.h, part.cpp, processor.h, processor.cpp, memory.h, memory.cpp, hdisk.h, hdisk.cpp, cd.h, cd.cpp, fdisk.h, fdisk.cpp, keyboard.h, keyboard.cpp, montior.h, monitor.cpp, mouse.h, and mouse.cpp. Save your program as Ch4-ip2.cpp in the Chapter4 folder.

More on Inheritance

Introduction ▶ In this chapter, you will learn about topics related to reusing a class after you implement it, including using different types of inheritance (public, private, and protected), creating virtual functions (methods), and creating virtual base classes. You also will study the differences between static binding and dynamic binding, and learn how to request dynamic binding in C++ programs. Finally, you will learn about abstract base classes and base class pointers.

Types of Derivation

In Chapter 4, you used the keyword `public` to use inheritance when deriving a new class from an existing class. Three different types of derivation are available to C++ programmers: `public`, `private`, and `protected`. Your choice of a derivation type dictates how inherited members will appear in the derived class (`public`, `private`, or `protected`).

Public, Private, and Protected Members

Syntax ▶

```
class Classname
{
  public:    // Public members
  protected: // Protected members
  private:   // Private members
};
```

Earlier, you learned that public class members provide the interface to the class, which means that the public members are available to the class's user. Although private class members remain inaccessible to the class's user, they are accessible to the public class members. As a consequence, the user of the class must use the inherited public members to gain access to the private members. New methods added to a derived class do not have access to the inherited private members.

Protected access is a new concept introduced in this chapter. If class members are protected, class members and class members of derived classes can access them. That is, in a derived class, new methods added to the derived class will be able to access the protected members inherited from the base class.

Public, Private, and Protected Derivations

Syntax ▶

```
class derived_class_name : derivation type base_class_name
```

In Chapter 4, you created derived classes using public derivation. Example 5-1 shows a class derivation using protected derivation.

Example 5-1 ▶

```
class Video_Machine : protected Video
{
    . . .  // Public, private, and protected members
};
```

The derivation type that you request when creating a derived class determines how the derived class receives inherited members. Figure 5-1 lists the three derivation types, the base class member's access type, and the access available to the derived class.

Derivation Type	Base Class Member Access	Derived Class Access
private	private	inaccessible
	public	private
	protected	private
public	private	inaccessible
	public	public
	protected	protected
protected	private	inaccessible
	public	protected
	protected	protected

Figure 5-1: Derivation types

As shown in Figure 5-1, a **private derivation** results in a derived class that has:

■ Inherited private data members from the base class that are inaccessible in the derived class
■ Inherited public members and protected members from the base class that are private members in the derived class

A **public derivation** results in a derived class that has:

■ Inherited private data members from the base class that are inaccessible in the derived class
■ Inherited public members from the base class that are public members in the derived class
■ Inherited protected members from the base class that are protected members in the derived class

A **protected derivation** results in a derived class that has:

■ Inherited private data members from the base class that are inaccessible in the derived class
■ Inherited public members and protected members from the base class that are protected members in the derived class

As shown in Figure 5-1, private class members are always inaccessible to a derived class. Thus, you must use inherited methods to access them from within the derived class. Any new methods that you write for the derived class will not have access to these members; therefore, they must use the inherited base class methods.

Deriving Classes

Using protected access provides a way for class members to behave as private members in the base class and still remain accessible in derived classes. New methods written for the derived class will have access to the inherited members because they are protected, rather than private. Users of the derived class do not have access to protected members; they must access them through the use of methods, in the same way that private members are accessed. Example 5-2 shows the class declaration for a base class named `Mailing_Info`. Examples 5-3, 5-4, and 5-5 show three derived classes named `Employee`, `Vendor`, and `Client`. The `Employee`, `Vendor`, and `Client` classes have been derived using different derivation types.

Example 5-2 ▶

```
// mailing_info.h - not on Student Disk
#ifndef MAILING_INFO_H
#define MAILING_INFO_H
const int SIZE = 30;
class Mailing_Info
{
public:
  void print()const;
  Mailing_Info();
  ~Mailing_Info();
protected:
  const char* get_name()const;
  char address[SIZE];
  char city[SIZE];
  char state[SIZE];
  char zip[SIZE];
private:
  char name[SIZE];
};
#endif
```

The `Mailing_Info` class has three public members: a `print()` method, a constructor, and a destructor. The `Mailing_Info` class has five protected members: the data members `address`, `city`, `state`, and `zip`, and the `get_name()` method. The `Mailing_Info` class also has one private data member—`name`.

Example 5-3 ▶

```
// employee.h - not on Student Disk
#ifndef EMPLOYEE_H
#define EMPLOYEE_H
#include "mailing_info.h"
// Protected derivation
class Employee : protected Mailing_Info
{
public:
  // Other public members
  void send_paycheck()const;
private:
  double pay_rate;
  short hours_worked;
};
#endif
```

Example 5-3 shows the `Employee` class that is derived from the `Mailing_Info` class by using the protected derivation type. The public member of the `Mailing_Info` class (the `print()` method) will, therefore, be a protected member in the derived class. The protected members of the `Mailing_Info` class (address, city, state, zip, and get_name()) also will be protected members in the derived class. The send_paycheck() method in the derived class (Employee), therefore, has access to the data members address, city, state, and zip and the methods get_name() and print() because they are protected members in the newly derived Employee class. The derived Employee class does not have access to name because it was a private data member in the base class Mailing_Info; therefore, name is inaccessible in the derived class.

Example 5-4 ▶

```
// client.h - not on Student Disk
#ifndef CLIENT_H
#define CLIENT_H
#include "mailing_info.h"
class Client : private Mailing_Info  // Private derivation
{
public:
  void send_bill()const;
private:
  double balance;
};
#endif
```

Example 5-4 shows the Client class that is derived from the Mailing_Info class by using the private derivation type. The public member of the Mailing_Info class (the print() method) will, therefore, be a private member in the derived class. The protected members of the Mailing_Info class (address, city, state, and zip and the get_name() method) will be private in the derived class. The send_bill() method in the derived class (Client), therefore, has access to the data members address, city, state, and zip and to the methods get_name() and print() because they are private members in the newly derived Client class. The derived Client class does not have access to name because it was a private data member in the base class Mailing_Info; therefore, name is inaccessible in the derived class.

Example 5-5 ▶

```
// vendor.h — not on Student Disk
#ifndef VENDOR_H
#define VENDOR_H
const int INV_SIZE = 20;
#include "mailing_info.h"
class Vendor : public Mailing_Info  // Public derivation
{
public:
  void pay_invoice()const;
private:
  double invoice_amount;
  char invoice_number[INV_SIZE];
};
#endif
```

Example 5-5 shows the Vendor class that is derived from the Mailing_Info class by using the public derivation type. The public member of the

Mailing_Info class (the print() method) will, therefore, be a public member in the derived class. The protected members of the Mailing_Info class (address, city, state, and zip) will be protected in the derived class. The pay_invoice() method in the derived class (Vendor), therefore, has access to the data members address, city, state, and zip and to the get_name() method because they are protected members in the newly derived Vendor class. The print() method is also accessible because it is a public member in the derived class. The derived Vendor class does not have access to name because it was a private data member in the base class Mailing_Info; therefore, name is inaccessible in the derived class.

Exercise 5.1 ▶

Joe Fleeting, the owner of the Time-Is-Right store, sells watches and alarm clocks. He has asked you to write a C++ program that will simulate setting and displaying the time and setting and displaying the band type for a watch as well as setting and displaying the time, setting the alarm, and hitting the snooze button for an alarm clock. Your program is saved as Ch5-1.cpp and your class files are saved as timepiece.h, timepiece.cpp, watch.h, watch.cpp, alarm.h, and alarm.cpp in the Chapter5 folder on your Student Disk. Change all private members to protected in the class files, and then make any appropriate changes to other class members. Save your changes in files named Ch5-1a.cpp, timepiecea.h, timepiecea.cpp, watcha.h, watcha.cpp, alarma.h, and alarma.cpp in the Chapter5 folder.

Exercise 5.2 ▶

You have written a C++ program to simulate the operation of various aircraft, which you saved as Ch5-2.cpp in the Chapter5 folder on your Student Disk. This program uses Helicopter and Airplane objects. The class files for helicopters and airplanes are named helicopter.h, helicopter.cpp, airplane.h, and airplane.cpp in the Chapter5 folder. You derived the Helicopter and Airplane classes from the Aircraft class whose files are named aircraft.h and aircraft.cpp. Your program does not compile, however, so you do not know whether it runs correctly. Do not change the Ch5-2.cpp file to make the program work. Instead, change the .h and .cpp files for the classes so that the program runs correctly. Save your changes in files named helicoptera.h, helicoptera.cpp, airplanea.h, airplanea.cpp, aircrafta.h, and aircrafta.cpp in the Chapter5 folder.

Exercise 5.3 ▶

Write a C++ program that manages information about zoo animals. Your program should store the name (such as Polly or Stripes), weight, and age of each zoo animal and print this information. In addition, it should manage, store, and display the type (such as parrot) and wing span for each bird, and the type (such as tiger) and running speed for each feline. Derive the Bird and Feline classes from the ZooAnimal class using a private derivation. Put all data members for all classes in the protected section of the class declarations. When you have finished, save your program as Ch5-3a.cpp and your class files as zooa.h, zooa.cpp, birda.h, birda.cpp, felinea.h, and felinea.cpp in the Chapter5 folder on your Student Disk.

Static and Dynamic Binding

Static binding refers to the compiler's ability to select and invoke the correct function based on the function's signature. A function's **signature** includes the function's class, name, number of arguments it receives, and data types of the arguments. Static binding also is called **compile time binding**, because the compiler has enough information at compile time to select the correct function. Static binding is the default in C++.

Dynamic binding, on the other hand, is the ability to delay binding a function call until run time; for this reason, dynamic binding is also known as **run-time binding**. The programmer must request dynamic binding by using the keyword virtual. Later in this chapter, you will see the need for dynamic binding.

Base Class Pointers

Using the `Mailing_Info` class and the `Employee`, `Vendor`, and `Client` classes discussed in the previous section, you can see that to represent an entire mailing list, you probably would need to create an array of `Employee` objects, a separate array of `Vendor` objects, and yet another array of `Client` objects. By definition, an array is a collection of objects or data items that have the same data type—you can't create an array to hold all three different types of objects that make up your mailing list.

In C++, you can create a base class pointer. For example, you might create a pointer to a `Mailing_Info` object because `Mailing_Info` is the base class from which the `Employee`, `Vendor`, and `Client` classes are derived. Base class pointers offer an advantage in that you can use them to point to a base class object (such as a `Mailing_Info` object) or to point to a derived class object (such as an `Employee`, `Vendor` or `Client` object). You must derive the derived classes from the base class with a public derivation, however, because using a public derivation means that all the members of the base class are inherited—that is, what was public in the base class is also public in the derived class. Because the methods are usually public, the derived class will have the same public methods and therefore will behave like the base class, which allows you to write polymorphic functions. (Remember that polymorphic functions are functions that take many forms.) Now, you will be able to write functions that behave differently based on the object type to which the base class pointer points. Example 5-6 shows the revised `Mailing_Info` class; it now has a method named `mail_to()`, the `name` data member has been moved into the protected section, and the `get_name()` method has been deleted.

Example 5-6 ▶

```
// mailing_info.h
#ifndef MAILING_INFO_H
#define MAILING_INFO_H
const int A_SIZE = 30;
class Mailing_Info
{
public:
  void print()const;
  void mail_to()const;
  Mailing_Info(const char* = "", const char* = "",
               const char* = "", const char* = "",
               const char* = "");
protected:
  char name[A_SIZE];
  char address[A_SIZE];
  char city[A_SIZE];
  char state[A_SIZE];
  char zip[A_SIZE];
};
#endif

// mailing_info.cpp
#include "mailing_info.h"
#include <iostream.h>
#include <string.h>
```

```
Mailing_Info::Mailing_Info(const char* name_in,
  const char* addr_in, const char* city_in, const char* state_in,
  const char* zip_in)
{
  strcpy(name, name_in);
  strcpy(address, addr_in);
  strcpy(city, city_in);
  strcpy(state, state_in);
  strcpy(zip, zip_in);
}
void Mailing_Info::print() const
{
  cout << name << endl;
  cout << address << endl;
  cout << city  << endl;
  cout <<  state << endl;
  cout << zip << endl;
}
// Simulate addressing envelope
void Mailing_Info::mail_to() const
{
  cout << "In Mailing_Info mail_to() method." << endl;
  cout << name << endl;
  cout << address << endl;
  cout << city << ' ' <<  state << ' ' << zip << endl;
}
```

Now you can create the **Employee** class through inheritance by using a public derivation. Example 5-7 shows the **Employee** class.

Example 5-7 ▶

```
// employee.h
#ifndef EMPLOYEE_H
#define EMPLOYEE_H
#include "mailing_info.h"
// Public derivation
class Employee : public Mailing_Info
{
public:
  Employee(const char* = "", const char* = "",
           const char* = "", const char* = "",
           const char* = "", double = 0.0, short = 0);
  void calc_paycheck() const;
  void mail_to() const;
private:
  double pay_rate;
  short hours_worked;
};
#endif
```

```cpp
// employee.cpp
#include "employee.h"
#include <iostream.h>
// Constructor; also constructs base class Mailing_Info
Employee::Employee(const char* name_in, const char* addr_in,
    const char* city_in, const char* state_in,
    const char* zip_in, double pay_in,
    short hours_in):
Mailing_Info(name_in, addr_in, city_in, state_in, zip_in)
{
    pay_rate = pay_in;
    hours_worked = hours_in;
}
void Employee::calc_paycheck()const
{
    cout << pay_rate * hours_worked << endl;
}
void Employee::mail_to()const
{
    cout << "In Employee mail_to() method." << endl;
    // Calls calc_paycheck() method
    calc_paycheck();
    // Calls base class mail_to() method
    Mailing_Info::mail_to();
}
```

The `Employee` class inherits the methods `print()` and `mail_to()` from the base class `Mailing_Info`, as well as the data members `name`, `address`, `city`, `state`, and `zip`. Remember that these data members are accessible in the derived class. In the declaration of the `Employee` class, the `mail_to()` method is overwritten in the derived class to compute the check amount prior to mailing the paycheck to an employee. The base class `mail_to()` method is then called from within the derived class's `mail_to()` method.

Next, you can create the `Client` class by using the `Mailing_Info` class as the base class and a public derivation. Example 5-8 shows the `Client` class.

Example 5-8 ▶

```cpp
// client.h
#ifndef CLIENT_H
#define CLIENT_H
#include "mailing_info.h"
class Client : public Mailing_Info  // Public derivation
{
public:
    Client(const char* = "", const char* = "",
            const char* = "", const char* = "",
            const char* = "", double = 0.0);
    void calc_bill() const;
    void mail_to() const;
private:
    double balance;
};
#endif
```

```
// client.cpp
#include "client.h"
#include <iostream.h>
//Constructor; also constructs base class Mailing_Info
Client::Client(const char* name_in, const char* addr_in,
  const char* city_in, const char* state_in,
  const char* zip_in, double bal_in):
  Mailing_Info(name_in, addr_in, city_in,
               state_in, zip_in)
{
  balance = bal_in;
}
void Client::calc_bill() const
{
  cout << balance << endl;
}
void Client::mail_to() const
{
  cout << "In Client mail_to() method." << endl;
  // Invokes calc_bill() method
  calc_bill();
  // Invokes base class mail_to() method
  Mailing_Info::mail_to();
}
```

The `Client` class inherits the methods `print()` and `mail_to()` from the base class `Mailing_Info`, as well as the data members `name`, `address`, `city`, `state`, and `zip`. Remember that these data members are accessible in the derived class. In the declaration of the `Client` class, the `mail_to()` method is overwritten in the derived class to manage some of the details of mailing a bill to a client. The base class `mail_to()` method is then called from within the derived class's `mail_to()` method.

Now you are ready to use the base class and the derived classes. The C++ program shown in Example 5-9 takes advantage of an array of base class pointers. To run the following example program, you must compile four files—Ex5-9.ccp, client.ccp, employee.ccp, and mailing_info.ccp—to create a single executable file.

Example 5-9 ▶

```
//  Ex5-9.cpp
#include "mailing_info.h"
#include "employee.h"
#include "client.h"
const int M_SIZE = 50;
int main()
{
  // Array of base class pointers
  Mailing_Info*  mailing_list[M_SIZE];
  // Mailing_Info object
  mailing_list[0] = new Mailing_Info("Carolyn",
    "111 First Street", "Anycity",
    "AnyState", "11111"");
```

```
    // Employee object
    mailing_list[1] = new Employee("Laura",
      "222 Second Street", "Anycity",
      "AnyState", "22222", 20.00, 40);
    // Client object
    mailing_list[2] = new Client("Greg",
      "333 Third Street","Anycity","AnyState",
      "33333", 45000.00);
    // Which mail_to() method???
    mailing_list[0]->mail_to();
    // Which mail_to() method???
    mailing_list[1]->mail_to();
    // Which mail_to() method???
    mailing_list[2]->mail_to();
    // More processing takes place here
    return 0;
}
```

Output:

```
In Mailing_Info mail_to() method.
Carolyn
111 First Street
Anycity AnyState 11111
In Mailing_Info mail_to() method.
Laura
222 Second Street
Anycity AnyState 22222
In Mailing_Info mail_to() method.
Greg
333 Third Street
Anycity AnyState 33333
```

In Example 5-9, the answers to the questions "Which mail_to() method???" are always the `Mailing_Info` class `mail_to()` method, even though you did not want this to happen. You deliberately rewrote the `mail_to()` method in each of the derived classes `Employee` and `Client` so you could mail invoices to clients and paychecks to employees. Why, then, does the program call the incorrect `mail_to()`method? The answer involves static binding. Because you declared the array as an array of pointers to `Mailing_Info` objects, the compiler assumed that you would point to `Mailing_Info` objects. Therefore, it bound the function call to the `Mailing_Info` class's `mail_to()` method. You really need the compiler to wait until run time to see what the base class pointer points to—such as an `Employee`, `Client`, or `Mailing_Info` object—and then bind the function call to the appropriate method. In other words, you need dynamic binding. The next section shows how to accomplish dynamic binding by using virtual functions.

Virtual Functions (Methods)

To use dynamic binding instead of the default static binding, you include the keyword `virtual` before the function (method) declaration in the class declaration. For example, if you place the keyword `virtual` before the `mail_to()` method in the `Mailing_Info` class, the compiler will not bind calls to the `mail_to()` method at compile time but rather will wait until run time. When you make the `mail_to()` method become a virtual function in the base class, it will also become a virtual function in any derived classes. You do not have to use the keyword `virtual` in the derived class declarations. Example 5-10 shows the `Mailing_Info` class with a virtual function (method) named `mail_to()`.

Example 5-10 ▶

```cpp
// mailing_info_new.h
#ifndef MAILING_INFO_NEW_H
#define MAILING_INFO_NEW_H
const int A_SIZE = 30;
class Mailing_Info
{
public:
  void print() const;
  // Virtual function; request for dynamic binding
  virtual void mail_to() const;
  Mailing_Info(const char* = "", const char* = "",
               const char* = "", const char* = "",
               const char* = "");
protected:
  char name[A_SIZE];
  char address[A_SIZE];
  char city[A_SIZE];
  char state[A_SIZE];
  char zip[A_SIZE];
};
#endif
```

The C++ program shown in Example 5-11 will call the `Mailing_Info` class `mail_to()` method when the base class pointer points to a `Mailing_Info` object, the `Employee` class `mail_to()` method when the base class pointer points to an `Employee` object, and the `Client` class `mail_to()` method when the base class pointer points to a `Client` object. To run the following example program, you must compile four files—mailing_info_new.ccp, employee_new.ccp, and client_new.ccp—to create a single executable file.

Example 5-11 ▶

```cpp
// Ex5-11.cpp
#include "mailing_info_new.h"
#include "employee_new.h"
#include "client_new.h"
const int M_SIZE = 50;
int main()
{
  // Array of base class pointers
  Mailing_Info*  mailing_list[M_SIZE];
  // Mailing_Info object
  mailing_list[0] = new Mailing_Info("Carolyn",
    "111 First Street", "Anycity",
    "AnyState", "11111");
```

```
        // Employee object
        mailing_list[1] = new Employee("Laura",
          "222 Second Street", "Anycity",
          "AnyState", "22222", 20.00, 40);
        // Client object
        mailing_list[2] = new Client("Greg",
          "333 Third Street", "Anycity",
          "AnyState", "33333", 45000.00);
        // Mailing_Info mail_to() method
        mailing_list[0]->mail_to();
        // Employee mail_to() method
        mailing_list[1]->mail_to();
        // Client mail_to() method
        mailing_list[2]->mail_to();
        // More processing takes place here
        return 0;
}
```

Output:

```
In Mailing_Info mail_to() method.
Carolyn
111 First Street
Anycity AnyState 11111
In Employee mail_to() method.
800
In Mailing_Info mail_to() method.
Laura
222 Second Street
Anycity AnyState 22222
In Client mail_to() method.
45000
In Mailing_Info mail_to() method.
Greg
333 Third Street
Anycity AnyState 33333
```

Although dynamic binding is a powerful tool, you should remember that it uses additional resources and therefore reduces your program's performance.

Exercise 5.4 ▶

In Exercise 4.13 in Chapter 4, you developed a C++ program that used the Doctor and Staff classes, both of which were derived from the Employee class. The program read in data from the doctor.dat and staff.dat files. You stored the doctor.dat data in an array of Doctor objects and the staff.dat data in an array of Staff objects. Then you printed the doctors' names in alphabetical order by last name, as well as their salaries and areas of specialization. You also printed the staff members' names in alphabetical order by last name, as well as their salaries and job titles. In this exercise, you will rewrite this program to use an array of base class pointers that point to Doctor or Staff objects. Do not try to sort the array. For this exercise, print the names of all hospital employees (plus the salaries and fields of specialization for doctors and the salaries and job titles for staff members). You can use the C++ program saved as Ch5-4.cpp and the class files saved as employee.h, employee.cpp, doctor.h, doctor.cpp, staff.h, and staff.cpp in Chapter5 folder on your Student Disk or you can use your own solution to Exercise 4.13 (which appears in the Chapter4 folder). The data files doctor.dat and staff.dat are saved in the Chapter5 folder. Save your modifications as Ch5-4a.cpp, employeea.h, employeea.cpp, doctora.h, doctora.cpp, staffa.h, and staffa.cpp. in the Chapter5 folder.

Exercise 5.5

The program saved as Ch5-5.cpp in the Chapter5 folder on your Student Disk uses `Painting` and `Sculpture` objects to maintain the inventory for the Lost Worlds Museum. The `Painting` and `Sculpture` classes were derived from the `ArtObject` class. The class files are saved as art.h, art.cpp, painting.h, painting.cpp, sculpture.h, and sculpture.cpp in the Chapter5 folder. The museum's inventory is saved as painting.dat and sculpture.dat in the Chapter5 folder. The current version of the program reads in the data from the data files, and then uses an array of `ArtObject` pointers to point to dynamically allocated `Painting` or `Sculpture` objects. It does not print the data correctly, however. Find and fix the errors. Save your corrected program as Ch5-5a.cpp and the corrected class files as arta.h, arta.cpp, paintinga.h, paintinga.cpp, sculpturea.h, and sculpturea.cpp in the Chapter5 folder.

Exercise 5.6

The Big Bauble Jewelry Store has commissioned you to write a C++ program to maintain its inventory of rings, bracelets, and earrings. Create a `Jewelry` class to store each item's number, description (such as ring, earring, or bracelet), and price. Derive three new classes—`Ring`, `Earring`, and `Bracelet`—from this `Jewelry` class. Your program also needs to manage the size information for rings, clasp type information for bracelets, and style information (pierced or clip-on) for earrings. Use an array of base class pointers to represent the inventory and dynamically allocate memory for the objects. Read the inventory data from the file named jewelry.dat in the Chapter5 folder on your Student Disk. When you have finished, save your program as Ch5-6a.cpp and your class files as jewelrya.h, jewelrya.cpp, ringa.h, ringa.cpp, braceleta.h, braceleta.cpp, earringa.h, and earringa.cpp in the Chapter5 folder.

Inheriting the Implementation of a Class

In Chapter 4, you learned that a public derivation contains all of the base class members. The public members of the base class are public in the derived class, and the private members are inaccessible to methods written in the derived class. You can access the private members inherited from the base class by using the methods inherited from the base class. The derived class can then behave like the base class because it has inherited the base class's methods. The derived class also shares the base class's implementation because it inherits the base class's data members. In this way, public derivations allow you to create new classes that share both the behavior and implementation of the base class—this form of inheritance is the most used type.

In addition to creating classes that share the base class's behavior and implementation, you can create classes that share only the base class's implementation or only its behavior.

When you create a new class with inheritance by using private derivation, all public and protected members of the base class are private in the derived class, which means that they remain unavailable to users of the new class. When the members are unavailable, you actually block the user from using the behavior that was defined in the base class. On the other hand, you can write methods for the derived class that can take advantage of the inherited behavior of the base class.

For example, a `List` class might have methods that put an integer at the beginning of the list (`put_first()`) and get an integer from the beginning of the list (`get_first()`). The `List` class might also have methods that add an integer at the end of the list (`put_last()`) and find an integer in the list (`find()`). Now imagine that you want to use the List class to implement a stack. When using a stack, you should be able to push an item on the top of the stack (the first item in the stack) and pop an item from the stack (retrieve the first item from the stack). If you use the List class as the base class and derive a Stack class from it using a public derivation, all of the methods—put_first(), get_first(), put_last(), and find()—are available to the derived class's user, which means that the user can use the put_last() method and would, therefore, violate the correct management of the stack. On the other hand, if you derive the Stack class from the List class by using a private derivation, the List class methods would be private and, therefore, unavailable to the class's user. In the Stack class, you could write two new methods—push() and pop()—and their implementations could use the inherited methods put_first(), get_first(), put_last(), and find(). This approach allows you to inherit the implementation of the List class but not its behavior. In other words, users of the Stack class cannot use the methods put_first(), get_first(), put_last(), or find(); they will be limited to using the methods push() and pop(). Example 5-12 shows the List and Stack class definitions and a C++ program that uses the List and Stack classes. To run the following example program, you must compile three files—Ex5-12.ccp, list.ccp, and stack.ccp—to create a single executable file.

Example 5-12 ▶

```cpp
// list.h
#ifndef LIST_H
#define LIST_H
class List
{
public:
  void put_first(int);
  int get_first() const;
  void put_last(int);
  int find(int) const;
private:
  // Implementation details go here
};
#endif

// stack.h
#ifndef STACK_H
#define STACK_H
#include "list.h"
// Private derivation
class Stack : private List
{
public:
  void push(int);
  int pop() const;
private:
  // Additional private members would go here
};
#endif

// stack.cpp
#include "stack.h"
void Stack::push(const int val)
{
```

```
    List::put_first(val);
}
int Stack::pop() const
{
    return List::get_first();
}

// Ex5-12.cpp
#include "list.h"
#include "stack.h"
int main()
{
    List list;
    Stack stack;
    int value;

    list.put_first(15);         // Legal
    list.put_last(20);          // Legal
    value = list.get_first();   // Legal
    stack.push(22);             // Legal
    stack.push(25);             // Legal
    // stack.put_first(34);         Illegal
    // stack.put_last(55);          Illegal
    value = stack.pop();        // Legal
    return 0;
}
```

Output:

```
15 is now the first item in the list.
20 is now the last item in the list.
Returning first integer in the list.
22 is now the first item in the list.
25 is now the first item in the list.
Returning first integer in the list.
```

Exercise 5.7 ▶   On a piece of paper, write the class declaration for a new class named Queue that you should derive from the List class used in Example 5-12. Derive the Queue class so that it inherits the implementation of the List class but not its behavior. The Queue class should contain the behaviors that are legal to maintain a queue, to enqueue (that is, to place an item at the rear of the queue), and to dequeue (that is, to delete an item from the front of the queue). Also, write the enqueue() and dequeue() methods and a C++ program similar to the one shown in Example 5-12 that uses your new Queue class.

Inheriting the Behavior of a Class

In C++, you can derive a class from an existing class so that the derived class will inherit the behavior of the base class but not its implementation. The base class and the derived class will, therefore, have similar sets of methods but will be implemented in totally different ways. For example, you can create a base class for a Shape that will contain several pure virtual functions (methods), such as draw() and rotate(), that indicate which behaviors to define for any type of Shape. A **pure virtual function** is simply a virtual function that has no code written for it, but instead is initialized with zero. As a virtual function, it obeys the rules of dynamic binding and waits until run time to determine which `draw()` or `rotate()` method to invoke. You must write the code in the derived class to specify what it means to draw a circle, square, or diamond. In other words, you must rewrite pure virtual functions for any class that is derived from a class that contains a pure virtual function. Therefore, all of the derived classes will have the same methods (behaviors) defined and will inherit the behavior of the base class. The implementation of the base class, however, is not inherited.

Any class that contains a pure virtual function is called an **Abstract Base Class**. You cannot instantiate objects from an Abstract Base Class; Abstract Base Classes are written solely for the purpose of inheritance. Example 5-13 shows the class declaration for the `Shape` class, which is an Abstract Base Class.

Example 5-13 ▶

```
// shape.h
#ifndef SHAPE_H
#define SHAPE_H
class Shape
{
public:
  // Pure virtual function
  virtual void draw() const = 0;
  // Pure virtual function
  virtual void rotate(int) const = 0;
private:
  // No private data members
};
#endif
```

If you derive the `Circle` class from the Abstract Base Class (`Shape`), you must rewrite the `draw()` and `rotate()` methods. If you derive a `Rectangle` class from the `Shape` class, you must rewrite the `draw()` and `rotate()` methods for the `Rectangle` class as well. The Abstract Base Class (`Shape`) dictates the behaviors that must be written for the derived classes. Although the interface (behaviors) has been inherited from the base class, the implementation details will vary according to the type of shape that is drawn or rotated. Example 5-14 shows the `Rectangle` class that is derived from the Abstract Base Class (`Shape`). To run the following example program, you must compile two files—Ex5-14.ccp and rectangle.ccp—to create a single executable file.

Example 5-14 ▶

```
// rectangle.h
#ifndef RECTANGLE_H
#define RECTANGLE_H
#include "shape.h"
class Rectangle: public Shape
{
public:
  Rectangle(int, int);
  // Rewritten pure virtual function
  void draw() const;
  // Rewritten pure virtual function
  void rotate(int) const;
```

```cpp
private:
  int length;   // Length of rectangle
  int width;    // Width of rectangle
};
#endif

// rectangle.cpp
#include "rectangle.h"
#include <iostream.h>
Rectangle::Rectangle(int length_in, int width_in)
{
  length = length_in;
  width = width_in;
}
void Rectangle::draw() const
{
  int j, k;
  for(j = 0; j < width; j++)
    cout << '-';
  cout << endl;
  for(j = 0; j < length - 2; j++)
    for(k = 0; k < width; k++)
      if(k == 0)
        cout << '-';
      else if(k == width - 1)
        cout << '-' << endl;
      else
        cout << ' ';
  for(j = 0; j < width; j++)
    cout << '-';
  cout << endl;
}
void Rectangle::rotate(int degrees) const
{
  cout << "Rotating rectangle " << degrees << " degrees."
       << endl;
}
// Other methods

// Ex5-14.cpp
#include "rectangle.h"
int main()
{
  Rectangle rect1(8,4);
  rect1.draw();
  rect1.rotate(30);
  return 0;
}
```

Output:

```
----
-  -
-  -
-  -
-  -
-  -
----
Rotating rectangle 30 degrees.
```

You can create nearly any `Shape`. The implementation of a circle has different requirements, however. First, you need a data member for the radius of the circle, and *x*- and *y*-coordinates for the circle's center. You must then rewrite the `draw()` and `rotate()` methods for the `Circle` class using the implementation details (data members) of the `Circle` class.

Exercise 5.8 ▶ On a piece of paper, write the class declaration for a new class named `Horizontal_Line`. Derive the `Horizontal_Line` class from the `Shape` class used in this section. Derive the `Horizontal_Line` class so that it inherits the behavior of the `Shape` class but not its implementation. In addition to the class declaration, write the `draw()` method for the `Horizontal_Line` class.

Multiple Class Inheritance

Syntax ▶ class derived_class: derivation class_name, derivation class_name

You can derive a C++ class from more than one base class; this concept is known as **multiple inheritance**. To derive a class from two base classes, you include the names of both classes in a comma-separated list when writing the declaration for the derived class. You have already used objects that belong to classes that have been derived using multiple inheritance. For example, the `cin` and `cout` objects are `iostream` instantiations. The `iostream` class has been derived from two classes, `istream` and `ostream`. The `istream` and `ostream` classes have been derived from a class named `ios`. Figure 5-2 illustrates this class hierarchy. You will learn more about these classes in Chapter 6.

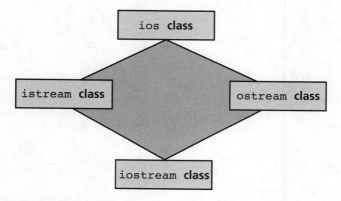

Figure 5-2: Hierarchy for `iostream` class

For example, suppose that you want to write a `TelephoneAnsMachine` class that is derived from two classes: `Phone` and `AnsweringMachine`. Example 5-15 shows the class declaration for the `Phone` class, and Example 5-16 shows the class declaration for the `AnsweringMachine` class.

Example 5-15 ▶

```
// phone.h
#ifndef PHONE_H
#define PHONE_H
class Phone
{
public:
  void display() const;  // Display phone number dialed
  // Other methods
protected:
  // Data members
};
#endif
```

Example 5-16 ▶

```
// ans_machine.h
#ifndef ANS_MACHINE_H
#define ANS_MACHINE_H
class AnsweringMachine
{
public:
  void display() const; // Displays number of messages recorded
  // Other methods
protected:
  // Data members
};
#endif
```

Because a telephone answering machine is both a telephone *and* an answering machine, you can use multiple inheritance to create the `TelephoneAnsMachine` class by deriving it from the `Phone` class and the `AnsweringMachine` class. Example 5-17 shows the declaration for the `TelephoneAnsMachine` class.

Example 5-17 ▶

```
// tel_ans_mach.h
#ifndef TEL_ANS_MACH_H
#define TEL_ANS_MACH_H
#include "phone.h"
#include "ans_machine.h"
class TelephoneAnsMachine: public Phone, public AnsweringMachine
{
public:
  TelephoneAnsMachine();  // Default constructor
  // Displays phone number dialed and number of messages recorded
  void display_all_data() const;
protected:
  // Add new data members here
};
#endif
```

Because the `TelephoneAnsMachine` class was publicly derived from the `Phone` and the `AnsweringMachine` classes, the public members of the two classes are public in the derived class and the protected members of the two classes are protected in the derived class. As shown in Example 5-18, a newly created `TelephoneAnsMachine` object might invoke the `display_all()` method, the `display()` method inherited from the `Phone` class, or the `display()` method inherited from the `AnsweringMachine` class. To run the following example program, you must compile four files—Ex5-18.ccp, phone.ccp, ans_machine.ccp, and tel_ans_machine.ccp—to create a single executable file.

Example 5-18 ▶

```cpp
// Ex5-18.cpp
#include "tel_ans_mach.h"

int main()
{
  // Creates an object
  TelephoneAnsMachine my_ans_mach;
  // Calls the TelephoneAnsMachine method
  my_ans_mach.display_all_data();
  // my_ans_mach.display();   Compiler error; ambiguous

  return 0;
}
```

As you might guess, you have created a problem in your derived class. When a `TelephoneAnsMachine` object invokes the `display()` method, which `display()` method will be called? Actually, this situation will generate a compiler error because the compiler will not be able to determine which `display()` method to call: the one inherited from the `Phone` class or the one inherited from the `AnsweringMachine` class. To fix the problem, you must explicitly name the class to which the `display()` method belongs in conjunction with using the scope resolution operator (`::`), as shown in Example 5-19. To run the following example program, you must compile four files—Ex5-19.ccp, phone.ccp, ans_machine.ccp, and tel_ans_machine.ccp—to create a single executable file.

Example 5-19 ▶

```cpp
// Ex5-19.cpp
#include "tel_ans_mach.h"

int main()
{
  // Creates an object
  TelephoneAnsMachine my_ans_mach;
  // Calls the TelephoneAnsMachine method
  my_ans_mach.display_all_data();
  // Calls Phone method
  my_ans_mach.Phone::display();
  // Calls AnsweringMachine method
  my_ans_mach.AnsweringMachine::display();

  return 0;
}
```

Output:

```
Displaying phone number dialed.
Displaying number of messages recorded.
Displaying phone number dialed.
Displaying number of messages recorded.
```

You also could write the `display_all_data()` method for the `TelephoneAnsMachine` class as shown in Example 5-20.

Example 5-20 ▶

```
// tel_ans_mach.cpp
#include "tel_ans_mach.h"
#include <iostream.h>
// Other methods
void TelephoneAnsMachine::display_all_data()
{
  // Invokes Phone method
  Phone::display();
  // Invokes AnsweringMachine method
  AnsweringMachine::display();
}
```

Although solving the problems introduced by multiple inheritance is not diffi-cult, you should use this technique sparingly. Many object-oriented programmers will insist that you should *never* use multiple inheritance. In fact, languages such as Java and SmallTalk do not support multiple inheritance.

Virtual Base Classes

You now understand how to use inheritance to derive a new class from a single base class or from multiple base classes. But what happens when you want to derive a new class from two classes that have been derived from the same base class? Figure 5-3 illustrates the class hierarchy that applies to this situation.

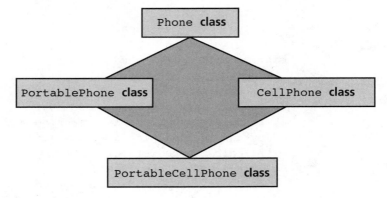

Figure 5-3: Class hierarchy

As shown in Figure 5-3, the `Phone` class is the base class. Both the `PortablePhone` and `CellPhone` classes have been derived from the `Phone` class, which means that both classes inherit the members of the `Phone` class. The `PortableCellPhone` class is derived from both the `PortablePhone` and `CellPhone` classes. Therefore, the `PortableCellPhone` class will contain two copies of the members of the `Phone` class. You can prevent the duplication of the `Phone` class members by using the keyword `virtual` to specify that the base class (`Phone`) should be included only once. When you use the `virtual` keyword in this way, you are taking advantage of a Virtual Base Class. Example 5-21 shows the class declarations for the `Phone`, `PortablePhone`, `CellPhone`, and `PortableCellPhone` classes and demonstrates the use of the keyword `virtual` to avoid the problem of including duplicate class members.

Example 5-21 ▶

```
// phone.h - not on Student disk
#ifndef PHONE_H
#define PHONE_H
class Phone
{
  // Phone class members
};
#endif


// Using virtual in the following class declaration
// makes Phone a virtual base class.
// portable.h — not on Student Disk
#ifndef PORTABLE_H
#define PORTABLE_H
class PortablePhone: virtual public Phone
{
  // PortablePhone class members
  // PortablePhone class also inherits members
  // of the Phone class.
};
#endif


// Using virtual in the following class declaration
// makes Phone a virtual base class.
// cell.h — not on Student Disk
#ifndef CELL_H
#define CELL_H
class CellPhone: virtual public Phone
{
  // CellPhone class members
  // CellPhone class inherits members
  // of the Phone class.
};
#endif


// port_cell_phone.h — not on Student Disk
#ifndef PORT_CELL_PHONE_H
#define PORT_CELL_PHONE_H
class PortableCellPhone: public PortablePhone, public CellPhone
{
```

```
// PortableCellPhone class members
// PortableCellPhone class inherits members
// of the PortablePhone class and inherits members
// of the CellPhone class.
// PortablePhone and CellPhone are both derived
// from the Phone class, so the PortableCellPhone class
// would inherit duplicate copies of the members
// of the Phone class if the keyword virtual
// was omitted from the class declaration for
// PortablePhone and CellPhone.
};
#endif
```

When you use a virtual base class, remember that the class furthest down in the hierarchy must construct the base class. In Example 5-21, the responsible class is the `PortableCellPhone` class. Using the `virtual` keyword allows the `PortablePhone` and `CellPhone` classes not to worry about the construction of their parent. If the `PortablePhone` and `CellPhone` classes were responsible for constructing their parent, you would end up with the duplication that you sought to avoid by using the `virtual` keyword. For example, suppose that the `Phone` class requires values for `tel_number` and `area_code`, the `PortablePhone` class requires a value for `battery_size`, the `CellPhone` class requires a value for `cell_num`, and the `PortableCellPhone` class requires a value for `id_num`. You would then need to write the `PortableCellPhone` constructor to construct all of the classes. Example 5-22 shows the constructor for the `PortableCellPhone` class.

Example 5-22 ▶

```
PortableCellPhone(const int tel_num, const short a_code,
  const short bat_size, const short c_num,
  const short id):
  id_num(id), Phone(tel_num, a_code),
  PortablePhone(bat_size), CellPhone(c_num)
{
}
```

Exercise 5.9 ▶

The C++ program saved as Ch5-9.cpp in the Chapter5 folder on your Student Disk uses `Breakfast`, `Lunch`, and `Brunch` objects to represent the menu items served at the Rise and Shine Restaurant. The Rise and Shine Restaurant serves a brunch only on Sundays. Your C++ program will not run until you derive a new `Brunch` class that is derived from the `Breakfast` and `Lunch` classes and represents the menu items that will be available for the Sunday brunch. Derive the new `Brunch` class and then run the C++ program. Save your new class files as brunch.h and brunch.cpp. The `Lunch` and `Breakfast` class files are saved as lunch.h, lunch.cpp, breakfast.h, and breakfast.cpp in the Chapter5 folder. When you have finished, the program should produce the following output:

```
Enter the name of the breakfast item: bacon
Enter the price of the breakfast item: 1.99
Breakfast item: bacon
Price: 1.99
Brunch item is actually a Breakfast item: bacon
Price: 1.99
Enter the name of the lunch item: sandwich
Enter the price of the lunch item: 3.99
```

```
Lunch item: sandwich
Price: 3.99
Brunch item is actually a Lunch item: sandwich
Price: 3.99
```

Exercise 5.10 ▶

You have invented a new writing instrument—one end is a pencil and the other end is an ink pen. You wrote a C++ program to simulate using your new writing instrument, which is saved as Ch5-10.cpp in the Chapter5 folder on your Student Disk. You created a base class named `WritingInstrument` and derived two classes—`Pen` and `Pencil`—from the `WritingInstrument` class. Then you derived the `PenPencil` class from the `Pen` and `Pencil` classes. Your program does not link correctly, however. Study the current version of the program and the class files to find the errors. The class files are saved as writing.h, pen.h, pen.cpp, pencil.h, pencil.cpp, penpencil.h, and penpencil.cpp in the Chapter5 folder. Make the necessary corrections, then save the files as Ch5-10a.cpp, writinga.h, pena.h, pena.cpp, pencila.h, pencila.cpp, penpencila.h, and penpencila.cpp in the Chapter5 folder.

Exercise 5.11 ▶

Write a C++ program that lets you create `SavingsAccount`, `CheckingAccount`, and `MoneyMarket` objects. Derive the `SavingsAccount` and `CheckingAccount` classes from a base class named `BankAccount`, and derive the `MoneyMarket` class from the `CheckingAccount` and `SavingsAccount` classes. All of the objects should be able to invoke the methods `deposit()` and `withdraw()`. A `CheckingAccount` object should be allowed to write a check, and a `SavingsAccount` object should be able to calculate its interest. A `MoneyMarket` object should be able to write a check and calculate its interest. When you have finished, save your program as Ch5-11a.cpp and your class files as banka.h, banka.cpp, savinga.h, savinga.cpp, checka.h, checka.cpp, moneya.h, and moneya.cpp in the Chapter5 folder on your Student Disk.

S U M M A R Y

- Public data members provide the interface to the users of a class. Private data members remain inaccessible to the users of a class—they must be accessed through public members. Protected data members may be accessed by both, their own class members and by class members of a derived class.

- There are three types of derivation: public, private, and protected. Your choice of a type of derivation when creating a derived class determines how the derived class receives inherited members.

- Static binding refers to the compiler's ability to choose the appropriate function to invoke based on the function's signature. This type of binding occurs at compile time and is the default in C++.

- Dynamic binding is the ability to postpone binding of a function call until run time. The programmer must request dynamic binding by using the keyword `virtual`.

- You can use base class pointers to point to a base class object or to a derived class object, if the derived class was derived as public from the base class.

- Base class pointers enable you to write polymorphic functions. Polymorphic functions will behave differently depending on the type of object to which the base class pointer points, and requires the use of virtual functions.

- Including the keyword `virtual` before the method declaration in the class declaration creates virtual functions. The keyword `virtual` alerts the compiler not to bind the function at compile time, but rather to wait until run time.

- It is possible to inherit the behavior and the implementation of a class (public derivation), just the implementation of a class (private derivation), or just the behavior of a class (pure virtual functions and Abstract Base Classes).

- A private derivation results in a derived class with the inherited members of the base class in the private section of the derived class, which makes the inherited members—even the methods—inaccessible to the class users. You can write methods for the derived class that use the inherited methods.
- A pure virtual function is a virtual function that has no code written for it but instead is initialized with zero, which forces you to rewrite the function in any classes derived from the base class. All derived classes will have the same methods defined; therefore, they will inherit the behavior of the base class.
- A class that contains any pure virtual functions is called an Abstract Base Class. You cannot create (instantiate) an object from an Abstract Base Class.
- In C++, you can derive a class from more than one class, a technique known as multiple inheritance. When using multiple inheritance, method names often must be resolved by using the scope resolution operator (::).
- A class that has been derived from multiple classes must provide for the construction of all base classes. When a class has been derived from two or more classes that have in turn been derived from the same base class, you can avoid duplication of the base class by using the keyword `virtual`, which ensures that the base class will be created only once.

PROGRESSIVE PROJECTS

1. Green Grocery Online Shopping Program

In Chapter 4, you created the `Inventory` class, which contained two data members: an array of `GroceryItem` objects and the `num_items` data member. The `num_items` data member contains the number of `GroceryItem` objects stored in the array. You also made the necessary modifications to your existing program and classes to use these data members.

In this chapter, do not use the completed project from Chapter 4. Instead, you will modify your project from Chapter 3. Change the private data members to protected data members in all of the classes, and then change any methods that are impacted by this change. Instead of an array of `GroceryItem` objects, create an array of base class pointers (pointers to `GroceryItem` objects). Populate this array with the data saved in the file named grocery.dat in the Chapter5 folder on your Student Disk. Derive five new classes from the `GroceryItem` class: `Dairy`, `Cereal`, `Bread`, `Jams`, and `Soup`. Add a virtual method named `print_order()` to the `GroceryItem` class that prints the string constant "Grocery Item" followed by the `item_name`, the `quantity_purchased`, and the dollar amount (`quantity_purchased * item_price`). The new classes should inherit the members of the `GroceryItem` class and add new methods to get and set the following information:

- `Dairy` objects: temperature
- `Cereal` objects: aisle number
- `Bread` objects: weight (in ounces)
- `Jam` objects: size (small, medium, or large)
- `Soup` objects: type (dry or liquid)

The new classes also should rewrite the virtual method `print_order()` to print the correct type of item. For example, when displaying a customer's order, the `print_order()` method should print the string constant "Bread" for a `Bread` object followed by the `item_name`, the `quantity_purchased`, and the dollar amount (`quantity_purchased * item_price`). Do not sort the array of base class pointers in this project.

When you have finished, save your program as Ch5-pp1.cpp in the Chapter5 folder on your Student Disk. Assign appropriate names to the .h and .cpp files for your classes.

2. Modified Five-Card Stud Poker

In Chapter 4, you created a `Player` class and modified the `Dealer` class. Both classes took advantage of composition to reuse existing classes. You also modified the `Card` class by storing the value of the `suit` member as an integer to facilitate determining the winning hand. In addition, you made all of the necessary modifications to your existing program and classes.

Because this project does not use inheritance, the topics covered in this chapter cannot be implemented in it. Instead, in this project you will calculate the winning hand. You will need to add data members to the `Player` class, such as `result` (to record the result of calculating a player's hand), `high_card` (the value of the highest card in a player's hand), `high_suit` (the value of the highest suit in a player's hand), `high_pair` (the value of the highest pair in a player's hand), and `high_three` (the value of the highest three-of-a-kind in a player's hand). These names are merely suggestions; you can add whatever data members you need to determine a winning hand. You also will add a `calc_hand()` method to determine the player's hand, and `get()` methods to retrieve the values of the added data members `result`, `high_card`, `high_suit`, `high_pair`, and `high_three`.

Consider the `calc_hand()` method carefully. You might use numeric values for the possible hands (straight flush = 9, four-of-a-kind = 8, and so on) to make determining the winning hand easier. Likewise, you might use the numeric values for suits (spades = 4, hearts = 3, diamonds = 2, and clubs = 1) to help determine a winning hand when a tie occurs. For example, if the first player has a straight flush and 10 is the highest card in the flush and the flush suit is spades, you can assign 9 to the `result` data member, 10 to the `high_card` data member, and 4 to the `high_suit` data member. If the second player has a pair of threes, you can assign 2 to the `result` and 3 to the `high_pair` data member. If the third player has an ace high card, you can assign 1 to the `result` and 14 to the `high_card` data member. If the fourth player has three fives, you can assign 4 to the `result` and 5 to the `high_three` data member.

If a tie occurs when determining the winning hand, you must check other values to determine a winner. For example, if two players each have a pair, check the high_pair data member to see which player has the highest pair.

When you have finished, save your program as Ch5-pp2.cpp in the Chapter5 folder on your Student Disk and your class files as player.h, player.cpp, dealer.h, and dealer.cpp, card.h, and card.cpp in the Chapter5 folder on your Student Disk.

INDEPENDENT PROJECTS

1. Remote Controls

In this project, you will simulate the operation of a remote control. Create a base class named RemoteControl that has the following data members: power (on or off), mute (on or off), and volume (a value from 1 to 10). Create a constructor and methods for the RemoteControl class that allow a user to turn the power on or off, turn the muting on or off, and increase or decrease the volume. Next, derive two classes from the RemoteControl class: TVRemote and VideoRemote. The TVRemote class should inherit the behavior and implementation of the RemoteControl class and have the data member channel_number (legal channels are 1 through 52). Include a method that handles changing channels. The VideoRemote class should inherit the behavior and implementation of the RemoteControl class and have the data members play (on or off), pause (on or off), and stop (on or off). Include methods that allow for playing, pausing, or stopping a video. When you have finished, save your program as Ch5-ip1.cpp in the Chapter5 folder on your Student Disk. Assign appropriate names to the .h and .cpp files for your classes.

2. Noah's Pet Emporium

Noah Arkstone, the owner of Noah's Pet Emporium, has commissioned you to write an inventory management system for his store, which sells dogs, cats, birds, and fish. The following information applies to every pet: pet_type (dog, cat, bird, or fish), age, weight, and price. In addition, the program should account for the breed and the type of food consumed (canned or dry) for dogs; the breed and claw status (clawed or declawed) for cats; the type (parrot, canary, and so on) and country of origin for birds; and the type (angel, neon, and so on) and water preference (salt or fresh) for fish. Your program should display all of the information for all pets, dogs only, cats only, birds only, and fish only. The inventory information appears in the file named noah.dat in the Chapter5 folder on your Student Disk.

Use public derivations and include a virtual function named display() in your base class that must be rewritten in each derived class. Use an array of base class pointers to represent the inventory so you can take advantage of dynamic binding.

When you have finished, save your program as Ch5-ip2.cpp in the Chapter5 folder on your Student Disk. Assign appropriate names to the .h and .cpp files for your classes.

Stream Input and Output

Introduction ▶ In this chapter, you will learn about the C++ stream classes. You will use the formatting flags and manipulators that are part of the **ios** class. In addition, you will use the members of the **istream** class to perform input operations, use the members of the **ostream** class to perform output operations, and use the members of the **fstream** class to accept input from and send output to files. Finally, you will learn how to overload the insertion and extraction operators for the classes that you create.

Stream Input/Output Library

A **stream** is a sequence of bytes. Different streams represent different types of data, depending on the class to which a stream object belongs. In the past, you have used the cin and cout objects of the istream and ostream classes. You also can use a stream object to represent a data file stored on a disk.

Using stream classes offers the following advantages:

- Simplicity—objects know how to display different data types without needing specific formatting instructions
- Overloading—you can create classes that include overloaded operators and methods, such as the extraction (>>) and insertion (<<) operators

C++ includes a hierarchy of stream classes. As shown in Figure 6-1, the ios class is the base class for the hierarchy. The istream and ostream classes are derived from the ios class. The iostream class is derived from both istream and ostream (an example of multiple class inheritance).

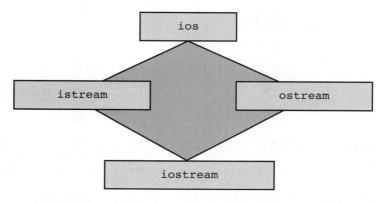

Figure 6-1: The ios class hierarchy

The ios Class

The **ios class** is the base class of the stream class hierarchy. As you know, a class consists of data members and methods. Formatting flags and error status bits are two members of the ios class.

Formatting Flags

Formatting flags enable you to specify formats for input and output. A C++ program can turn these flags on or off by using the methods setf() and unsetf(). Example 6-1 shows the C++ statements that turn on the left-justification flag, print text, and turn off the left-justification flag.

Example 6-1 ▶

```
cout.setf(ios::left);  // Turn on left justification
cout << "This text will be left-justified." << endl;
cout.unsetf(ios::left);  // Turn off left justification
```

As shown in Example 6-1, the flag's name (left) is preceded by the name of the class (ios) and the scope resolution operator.

Figure 6-2 describes the various ios formatting flags.

Flag	Meaning
skipws	Skips whitespace on input
left	Left-justify output
right	Right-justify output
dec	Convert output value to decimal (base 10)
oct	Convert output value to octal (base 8)
hex	Convert output value to hexadecimal (base 16)
showbase	Display O for octal and Ox for hexadecimal values
showpos	Display + before positive values
internal	Display padding (whitespace) between sign or base
showpoint	Display decimal point
scientific	Display E notation for floating point values
fixed	Display fixed format for floating point values
uppercase	Display an uppercase X (hex), E (scientific), A, B, C, D, E, F (hex values); default is lowercase

Figure 6-2: The ios class formatting flags

Formatting Methods

In addition to the setf() and unsetf() methods, several other methods belong to the ios class. Figure 6-3 describes these methods.

Method	Purpose
fill(ch);	Set fill character to ch; this character is printed in an unused part of a field
ch = fill();	Return current fill character
precision(p);	Set precision to p (number of places after decimal point)
p = precision();	Return current precision value
width(w);	Set field width to w
w = width();	Return current width value

Figure 6-3: Formatting methods

The C++ program in Example 6-2 uses the ios class format flags and class methods to specify formats for output values. The program's output is also shown.

Example 6-2 ▶

```cpp
// Ex6-2.cpp
#include <iostream.h>

int main()
{
  short age = 29;
  double salary = 45000.00;

  cout.setf(ios::left);  // Turn on left justification
  cout << age << endl;
  cout.unsetf(ios::left);  // Turn off left justification
  cout.width(10);  // Set field width to 10
  cout.setf(ios::right);  // Turn on right justification
  cout << age << endl;
  cout.unsetf(ios::right); // Turn off right justification

  cout.setf(ios::dec);  // Print value as base 10
  cout << age << endl;
  cout.setf(ios::oct);  // Print value as base 8
  cout << age << endl;
  cout.setf(ios::hex);  // Print value as base 16
  cout << age << endl;
  // Display value using uppercase letters
  cout.setf(ios::uppercase);
  cout << age << endl;

  cout.setf(ios::showbase);  // Show OX for hex
  cout << age << endl;
  cout.unsetf(ios::showbase);  // Turn off show OX for hex

  // Clear dec, oct, hex and then print value as base 10
  cout.setf(ios::dec, ios::basefield);

  cout.setf(ios::showpos);  // Show + sign
  cout << age << endl;

  cout.setf(ios::internal);  // Display padding
  cout << age << endl;

  cout.fill('*');  // Set fill character to '*'
  cout.width(10);  // Set field width to 10
  cout << age << endl;

  cout.setf(ios::showpoint);  // Display decimal point
  cout << salary << endl;

  cout.unsetf(ios::showpos);   // Turn off display of + sign
  cout.setf(ios::scientific);  // Display value in E notation
  cout << salary << endl;

  // Clear scientific format, then display value in fixed format
  cout.setf(ios::fixed, ios::floatfield);
  cout << salary << endl;
```

```
        cout.precision(2);   // Set precision
        cout << salary << endl;
        return 0;
}
```

Output:

```
29
        29
29
35
1d
1D
0X1D
+29
+29
+*******29
+45000.0
4.500000E+004
45000.000000
45000.00
```

Notice the C++ statement cout.setf(ios::dec, ios::basefield); in Example 6-2. This statement first clears the basefield, then turns on the dec flag. The use of basefield in this C++ statement clears all of the flags associated with printing values in different bases. Figure 6-4 shows other fields that you can clear using this same technique.

Flags to Turn On (First Argument)	Field to Clear (Second Argument)
dec, oct, hex	basefield
left, right, internal	adjustfield
scientific, fixed	floatfield

Figure 6-4: Using setf()with two arguments

Manipulators

Manipulators allow you to turn on many formatting flags. A **manipulator** is a format function that facilitates formatting tasks. You have already used a manipulator when you included endl in a cout statement. The endl manipulator inserts a newline character and flushes the stream.

C++ supports two types of manipulators: those that expect no arguments, and those that expect arguments. To use manipulators that expect arguments, you must #include <iomanip.h>. You do not need to do anything to use manipulators that do not expect arguments. Figure 6-5 lists the C++ manipulators that *do not* expect arguments; Figure 6-6 lists those manipulators that *do* expect arguments.

Manipulator	Meaning
ws	Skip whitespace (input)
endl	Insert newline and flush output stream
ends	Insert null character ('\0') to terminate a string
dec	Convert output value to decimal (base 10)
oct	Convert output value to octal (base 8)
hex	Convert output value to hexadecimal (base 16)
flush	Flush output stream

Figure 6-5: C++ manipulators with no arguments

Manipulator	Meaning
setw(int)	Set field width
setfill(int)	Set fill character (the default is a space)
setprecision(int)	Set precision (number of digits displayed after decimal point)
setiosflags(long)	Set flags
resetiosflags(long)	Clear flags

Figure 6-6: C++ manipulators with arguments

Example 6-3 shows a C++ program that uses some of these manipulators as well as the program's output.

Example 6-3 ▶

```
// Ex6-3.cpp
#include <iostream.h>
#include <iomanip.h>

int main()
{
  short age = 29;
  double salary = 45000.00;

  cout << setiosflags(ios::left);  // Turn on left justification
  cout << age << endl;
  // Turn off left justification
  cout << resetiosflags(ios::left);
  cout << setw(10);  // Set field width to 10
  // Turn on right justification
  cout << setiosflags(ios::right);
  cout << age << endl;
  // Turn off right justification
  cout << resetiosflags(ios::right);
```

```
        cout << setiosflags(ios::dec);   // Print value as base 10
        cout << age << endl;
        cout << setiosflags(ios::oct);   // Print value as base 8
        cout << age << endl;
        // Clear print value as base 8
        cout << resetiosflags(ios::oct);
        cout << setiosflags(ios::hex);   // Print value as base 16
        cout << age << endl;
        // Display value using uppercase letters
        cout << setiosflags(ios::uppercase);
        cout << age << endl;

        cout << setiosflags(ios::showbase);   // Show OX for hex
        cout << age << endl;
        // Turn off show OX for hex
        cout << resetiosflags(ios::showbase);

        // Turn off print value as base 16
        cout << resetiosflags(ios::hex);
        cout << setiosflags(ios::dec);   // Print value as base 10
        cout << setiosflags(ios::showpos);   // Show + sign
        cout << age << endl;

        cout << setiosflags(ios::internal);   // Display padding
        cout << age << endl;

        cout << setfill('*');   // Set fill character to '*'
        cout << setw(10);        // Set field width to 10
        cout << age << endl;

        cout << setiosflags(ios::showpoint);   // Display decimal point
        cout << salary << endl;

        // Turn off display of + sign
        cout << resetiosflags(ios::showpos);
        // Display value in E notation
        cout << setiosflags(ios::scientific);
        cout << salary << endl;

        // Clear ios::scientific
        cout << resetiosflags(ios::scientific);
        cout << setiosflags(ios::fixed);   // Display value as fixed
        cout << salary << endl;

        cout << setprecision(2);   // Set precision
        cout << salary << endl;
        return 0;
}
```

Output:

```
29
            29
29
35
1d
1D
0X1D
+29
+29
+*******29
+45000.0
4.500000E+004
45000.000000
45000.00
```

Stream Errors

The stream error status bits are members of the `ios` class. They represent errors that might occur during input or output operations. Figure 6-7 lists the names of the error status bits and their corresponding errors.

Status Bit	Error
goodbit	No errors (all bits off)
eofbit	End of file reached
failbit	Operation failed
badbit	Invalid operation
hardfail	Unrecoverable error

Figure 6-7: Error status bits

Several `ios` class methods are available to C++ programmers that read or clear the error bits. Figure 6-8 describes these methods.

Method	Meaning
eof();	Returns true (1) if eofbit is on
fail();	Returns true (1) if failbit, badbit, or hardfail bit is on
bad();	Returns true (1) if badbit or hardfail bit is on
good();	Returns true (1) if no bits are turned on
clear();	Clears all bits

Figure 6-8: Methods used with error bits

The C++ program shown in Example 6-4 uses the error bit methods to detect errors upon input.

Example 6-4 ▶

```
// Ex6-4.cpp
#include <iostream.h>
int main()
{
  short age;
  cout << "Enter your age: ";  // Get user input
  cin >> age;
  if(cin.good())  // Error status bit test - no errors
  {
    cin.ignore(256,'\n');  // Flush newline
    cout << "Age is " << age << '.' << endl;
  }
  else
  {
    cin.clear(); // Reset all bits to off
    cout << "Incorrect input, age must be an integer." << endl;
    cin.ignore(256,'\n');  // Flush input stream
  }
  return 0;
}
```

If the input is 20, then the output is:

`Age is 20.`

If the input is `twenty`, then the output is:

`Incorrect input, age must be an integer.`

Exercise 6.1 ▶

The `Video` class contains a `print()` method that prints each video's name, producer, and the quantity on hand. Rewrite the `print()` method so that the output is formatted as follows (the values for each video should print on separate lines):

Video Name (left-justified in a field width of 35)
Producer (left-justified in a field width of 35)
Quantity (right-justified in a field width of 10)

Test your new `print()` method by using the C++ program saved as Ch6-1.cpp in the Chapter6 folder on your Student Disk. The `Video` class files are saved as video.h and video.cpp in the same folder. Save your modified class files as videoa.h and videoa.cpp in the Chapter6 folder.

Exercise 6.2 ▶

The C++ program saved as Ch6-2.cpp in the Chapter6 folder on your Student Disk uses the `Rectangle` class to calculate the area and perimeter of a rectangle. You have decided to add some error-checking features to ensure that the input values are numeric values that your program can use in the calculations. In its current version, the program compiles but does not run correctly. The `Rectangle` class files are saved as rectangle.h and rectangle.cpp in the Chapter6 folder. Find and correct the errors, and then save your corrected files as rectanglea.h and rectanglea.cpp. You should not modify the Ch6-2.cpp file.

Exercise 6.3 ▶

Write a C++ program that prints the numeric value of the lowercase ASCII characters (a through z) in decimal (base 10), octal (base 8), and hexadecimal (base 16). Format your output as a table. Save the completed program as Ch6-3a.cpp in the Chapter6 folder on your Student Disk.

The `istream` Class

As noted earlier, the `istream` class is derived from the `ios` class. It therefore inherits the data members and methods that belong to the `ios` class. The `istream` class adds the ability to perform input and overloads the extraction operator (>>) to handle input of built-in data types such as int, char, float, double, and string.

In the past, you have used the `cin` object of the `istream` class type. The `cin` object represents the stream connected to the keyboard.

Figure 6-9 describes several methods that belong to the `istream` class.

Method	Meaning
>>	Extraction operator—provides formatted input for all built-in and overloaded user-defined types
get(ch);	Read one character and store in ch
get(str);	Read characters and store them in the character array str until '\n' is read
get(str, MAX);	Read up to MAX characters and store them in the character array str
get(str,MAX,DELIM);	Read characters and store them in the character array str until MAX characters or the DELIM character is read. The DELIM character is not extracted from the stream. The default delimiter is '\n'
getline(str,MAX,DELIM);	Read characters and store them in a character array str until MAX characters or the DELIM character is read. The DELIM character is extracted from the stream. The default delimiter is '\n'
putback(ch);	Return the last-read character to the input stream
ignore(MAX,DELIM);	Read and discard up to MAX characters, or until the DELIM character is read
peek(ch);	Read one character, but leave it in the input stream
clear();	Restore the input stream to a good state (turn error bits off)
read(str, MAX);	Read up to MAX characters from a file or until EOF is read, and then store in str

Figure 6-9: The `istream` class methods

Example 6-5 shows a C++ program that uses some of the `istream` class methods.

Example 6-5 ▶

```cpp
// Ex6-5.cpp
#include <iostream.h>
const int I_SIZE = 2;
const int N_SIZE = 30;
int main()
{
  char f_init, m_init, l_init[I_SIZE];
  char fname[N_SIZE], mname[N_SIZE], lname[N_SIZE];
  cout << "Enter your first initial: ";
  cin.get(f_init);  // Read one character and store in f_init
  cin.ignore(256,'\n');  // Read and discard newline character
  cout << "Enter your middle initial: ";
  cin >> m_init; // Read one character and store in m_init
  cin.ignore(256,'\n');  // Read and discard newline character
  cout << "Enter your last initial: ";
  // Read one character and store in l_init
  cin.get(l_init, I_SIZE);
  cin.ignore(256,'\n');  // Read and discard newline character
  cout << "Your initials are " << f_init << ' ' << m_init
       << ' ' << l_init << endl;
  cout << "Enter your first name: " ;
  // Read up to N_SIZE characters or newline
  cin.get(fname, N_SIZE);
  // Must read and discard newline character
  cin.ignore(256,'\n');
  cout << "Enter your middle name: ";
  // Newline character is extracted by getline()
  cin.getline(mname, N_SIZE);
  cout << "Enter your last name: ";
  // Read up to N_SIZE characters or newline
  cin.get(lname, N_SIZE, '\n');
  cout << "Your name is: " << fname << ' ' << mname << ' '
       << lname << endl;
  return 0;
}
```

The input to and output from this program are as follows:

```
Enter your first initial: J
Enter your middle initial: A
Enter your last initial: S
Your initials are J A S
Enter your first name: Mary
Enter your middle name: Clare
Enter your last name: Smith
Your name is: Mary Clare Smith
```

Exercise 6.4 ▶

The C++ program saved as Ch6-4.cpp in the Chapter6 folder on your Student Disk uses the Customer class. The Customer class files are saved as customer.h and customer.cpp in the Chapter6 folder. The Customer class currently has a single data member that stores each customer's first and last names. Change the program so that it stores each customer's first and last names in two separate data members. After you make the needed modifications, save the Customer class files as customera.h and customera.cpp. If you modify the Ch6-4.cpp program, save the revised file as Ch6-4a.cpp in the Chapter6 folder.

Exercise 6.5 ▶

The C++ program saved as Ch6-5.cpp in the Chapter6 folder on your Student Disk uses the `CustBalance` class. The `CustBalance` class files are saved as cust_bal.h and cust_bal.cpp in the Chapter6 folder. The program allows you to enter data to populate an array of `CustBalance` objects, and then prints the values stored in the array. Although the program compiles, it does not produce the correct output. Find and correct the errors, and then save your corrected files as cust_bala.h, cust_bala.cpp, and Ch6-5a.cpp in the Chapter6 folder.

Exercise 6.6 ▶

Write a C++ program that gets input and then stores that information in an array of 10 `Date` objects. Each `Date` object has three data members: `month` (a character string), `day` (a short), and `year` (a short). Your program should print the values stored in the 10 `Date` objects. Save the completed program as Ch6-6a.cpp and your class files as datea.h and datea.cpp in the Chapter6 folder on your Student Disk.

The `ostream` Class

As noted earlier, the `ostream` class is derived from the `ios` class. It therefore inherits the data members and methods of the `ios` class. The `ostream` class adds the ability to perform output operations and overloads the insertion operator (`<<`) to handle output of built-in data types such as int, char, float, double, and string.

In the past, you have used the `cout` object of the `ostream` class type. The `cout` object represents the stream connected to the screen display. Two other predefined `ostream` objects exist as well—`cerr`, which is used for error messages, and `clog`, which is used for log messages.

Figure 6-10 describes the methods that belong to the `ostream` class.

Method	Meaning
`<<`	Insertion operator; provides formatted output for all built-in and overloaded user-defined types
`put(ch);`	Write one character to the output stream
`flush();`	Flush output stream buffer and insert newline
`write(str,SIZE);`	Write up to `SIZE` characters from the array `str` to a file

Figure 6-10: The `ostream` class methods

Example 6-6 shows a C++ program that uses some of the `ostream` class methods.

Example 6-6 ▶

```
// Ex6-6.cpp
#include <iostream.h>
int main()
{
  char word[] = {"Programmer"};
  cout.put('U');   // Write one character to output stream
  cout << ' ';     // Write one character to output stream
  cout << 'R';     // Write one character to output stream
  cout.put(' ');   // Write one character to output stream
  cout << 'a';     // Write one character to output stream
```

```
    cout.put(' ');     // Write one character to output stream
    cout << "Good";    // Write string to output stream
    cout.put('\n');    // Write one character to output stream
    cout << word;      // Write string to output stream
    cout << endl;      // Use manipulator
    return 0;
}
```

Output:

```
U R a Good
Programmer
```

Exercise 6.7 ▶

The C++ program saved as Ch6-7.cpp in the Chapter6 folder on your Student Disk uses the `Time` class. The `Time` class files are saved as time.h and time.cpp in the Chapter6 folder. Compile and run this program, observing its output. Modify the program to use `ostream` methods and manipulators so as to produce tabular output. Save your modified program as Ch6-7a.cpp and the modified class files as timea.h and timea.cpp in the Chapter6 folder.

Exercise 6.8 ▶

For your Introduction to Computer Science class, you wrote a program that uses an `Arithmetic` class. This program reads two integers and one character that is either +, −, *, or / (representing the operations of addition, subtraction, multiplication, or division, respectively). The program should add, subtract, multiply, or divide the two integers, depending on the input character. It should output the first integer, the operator, the second integer, an = sign, and the result. The current version of this program does not compile, however. Find and correct the errors so that it generates the correct output. The program is saved as Ch6-8.cpp in the Chapter6 folder on your Student Disk, and the class files are saved as arithmetic.h and arithmetic.cpp in the Chapter6 folder. Save the completed program as Ch6-8a.cpp and the class files as arithmetica.h and arithmetica.cpp in the Chapter6 folder.

Exercise 6.9 ▶

Write a C++ program that draws a 4-by-4 character square. Draw the square using the # character and the `put()` method. Save the completed program as Ch6-9a.cpp in the Chapter6 folder on your Student Disk.

The `fstream` Class

Figure 6-11 shows an expanded stream class hierarchy that includes the `fstream` class and its ancestor classes. When you want to write data to or read data from a file, you can use the `fstream` class. As shown in Figure 6-11, the `fstream` class is derived from the `iostream` class, which descends from the `ios` class. This inheritance means that you can use the methods and manipulators discussed in the previous sections.

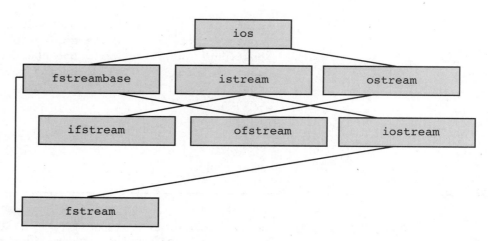

Figure 6-11: Stream class hierarchy

Simple File Input and Output

C++ programs can read their input from and write their output to a file. To use file input/output (I/O) in your C++ programs, you must:

- #include <fstream.h> at the beginning of your program
- Declare a file stream variable—for example, ifstream fin;, where ifstream is the class type for input files, or ofstream fout;, where ofstream is the class type for output files
- Open the input and/or output files using the open() method and specify the name of the file to open. For example:

```
fin.open("infile.dat");
fout.open("outfile.dat");
```

- Read the data stored in the input file or write data to the output file
- Close the input and/or output files using the close() method. For example:

```
fin.close();
fout.close();
```

When opening a file, you can use a second argument to indicate the file mode. Figure 6-12 describes the possible file modes.

Method	Meaning
ios::app	Append to the file
ios::ate	Position file pointer at the end of the file
ios::nocreate	File must exist or the open operation fails
ios::noreplace	File must not exist or the open operation fails

Figure 6-12: File modes

After you declare and open a file stream for your output file, you can write data to that file using the insertion operator (<<). Using the insertion operator with a file stream works in the same way as using it with the standard output stream (cout). You also can use any of the ostream methods mentioned in the previous section, such as put() and flush().

To read data from a file, you use the extraction operator (>>). Using the extraction operator with a file stream works in the same way as using it with the standard input stream (cin). You also can use any of the istream methods mentioned in the previous section, such as get(), getline(), putback(), ignore(), peek(), and clear().

The istream methods are used with a file input stream in the same way as they are used with the standard input stream (cin). For example, the following code instructs the ignore() method to read and discard up to 100 characters from the file input stream or to read and discard characters up to a newline character, whichever comes first:

```cpp
fin.ignore(100,'\n');
```

Using the following clear() method clears the file input stream:

```cpp
fin.clear();
```

You can use the close() method to close files when you no longer need them.

Example 6-7 shows a C++ program that performs input and output operations on a file.

Example 6-7 ▶

```cpp
// Ex6-7.cpp
#include <iostream.h>
#include <fstream.h>
#include <stdlib.h>
int main()
{
  ifstream fin;    // Input file stream
  ofstream fout;   // Output file stream
  char char_read;
  // Open input file
  fin.open("a:\\Chapter6\\Examples\\test_in.dat");
  if(!fin)  // Open failed
  {
    cerr << "Cannot open test_in.dat." << endl;
    exit(1);
  }
  // Open output file
  fout.open("a:\\Chapter6\\Examples\\test_out.dat");
  if(!fout)  // Open failed
  {
    cerr << "Cannot open test_out.dat." << endl;
    exit(2);
  }
  // Read one character; true until EOF is read
  while(fin >> char_read)
    // Write one character followed by a newline
    fout << char_read << endl;
  fin.close();   // Close input file
  fout.close();  // Close output file
  return 0;
}
```

When the contents of the input file, test_in.dat, are as follows:

```
This is a test file.
```

the output file will contain the following data:

```
T
h
i
s
i
s
a
t
e
s
t
f
i
l
e
.
```

File Output with Objects

```
ostream& write(char*, int);
```

The `write()` method allows you to write objects to a file. The first argument passed to the `write()` method is a pointer to a character that contains the address of the object to write to the file. You must typecast this argument because the address (pointer) is a pointer to an object—not a pointer to a character. The second argument is an integer that indicates the number of bytes to write or the size of the object.

The C++ statements in Example 6-8 create a `Video` object, open a file, and write the `Video` object to a file.

Example 6-8 ▶

```
ofstream fout;
Video rental;  // Video object
fout.open("a:\\Chapter6\\vid_out.dat");  // Open output file
// Statements to assign values to rental object
// Write Video object to file
fout.write((char*)&rental, sizeof(rental));
```

You can use the `write()` method in a loop to write an entire array of objects to a disk file. In Example 6-9, the C++ statements create an array of `Video` objects and write the objects stored in the array to a data file.

Example 6-9 ▶

```
#include "video.h"
#include <iostream.h>
const int SIZE = 50;
int main()
{
  ofstream fout;
  Video vid_inventory[SIZE];  // Array of Video objects
  int k;  // Loop counter
  fout.open("a:\\Chapter6\\vid_out.dat");  // Open output file
  // Statements to populate Video array with data
  for(k = 0; k < SIZE; k++)
    fout.write((char*)&vid_inventory[k],
              sizeof(vid_inventory[k])); // Write data
  return 0;
}
```

Example 6-10 shows an alternative technique to write the contents of an array in one statement.

Example 6-10 ▶

```
// You can write the contents of the array
// in one statement as follows:
fout.write((char*)&vid_inventory, sizeof(vid_inventory));
```

File Input with Objects

Syntax ▶

```
istream& read(char*, int);
```

You can read data from a file and populate an object with that data by using the **read()** method. The first argument passed to the **read()** method consists of a pointer to a character that contains the address of the object you want to populate with the data from the file. You must typecast this argument because the address of the object you are populating is a pointer to an object—not a pointer to a character. The second argument is an integer that indicates the number of bytes to read or the size of the object.

The C++ statements in Example 6-11 create a **Video** object, open an input file, and read data into the **Video** object.

Example 6-11 ▶

```
#include "video.h"
ifstream fin;
Video rental;  // Video object
fin.open("a:\\Chapter6\\vid_in.dat");  // Open input file
// Read values into rental object
fin.read((char*)&rental, sizeof(rental));
```

You can use the **read()** method in a loop to read data from an input file to populate an entire array of objects. In Example 6-12, the C++ statements create an array of **Video** objects and read data from an input file into the objects stored in the array.

Example 6-12 ▶

```
#include "video.h"
#include <iostream.h>
const int SIZE = 50;
int main()
{
  ifstream fin;
  Video vid_inventory[SIZE];   // Array of Video objects
  int k;                       // Loop counter
  fin.open("a:\\Chapter6\\vid_in.dat"); // Open input file
  for(k = 0; k < SIZE; k++)
    // Read data
    fin.read((char*)&vid_inventory[k],
             sizeof(vid_inventory[k]));
  // Alternatively, you can read data into an array of
  // objects using a single read() statement as follows:
  // fin.read((char*) &vid_inventory, sizeof(vid_inventory));
  return 0;
}
```

Exercise 6.10 ▶

The C++ program saved as Ch6-10.cpp in the Chapter6 folder on your Student Disk reads data from a file in the Chapter6 folder named players.dat. The data read are stored in an array of **Player** objects. After the program reads the data, it prints them to the screen. The program reads the data for each player until it reaches the end of file. Modify this program so that the data are read in one statement rather than in a loop. Save the modified program as Ch6-10a.cpp in the Chapter6 folder. The **Player** class files are saved as player.h and player.cpp in the Chapter6 folder.

Exercise 6.11 ▶

The C++ program saved as Ch6-11.cpp in the Chapter6 folder on your Student Disk reads data from a file named cd.dat, then stores those data in an array of **CD** objects. Each **CD** object contains a CD's name, recording artist, and price. After reading the data from cd.dat, the program interactively asks for the names, recording artists, and prices for additional CDs. These data are then added to the data file. The current version of the program does not add the new CD data to the file correctly. Find and fix the errors, then save your corrected program as Ch6-11a.cpp in the Chapter6 folder. *Note:* Make a copy of the data file cd.dat before beginning this exercise, because you will lose all existing data when you run the program. The **CD** class files are saved as cd.h and cd.cpp in the Chapter6 folder.

Exercise 6.12 ▶

Write a C++ program that copies an existing file. This program should prompt the user for any existing file's name as well as a name for the file's copy. It should not copy the file if the name specified for the copy is already in use. Save the completed program as Ch6-12a.cpp in the Chapter6 folder on your Student Disk.

Overloading the Insertion and Extraction Operators

Overloading the insertion (<<) and extraction (>>) operators is another stream-related feature of C++. This feature allows you to perform input and output operations for classes in the same way that you do for built-in data types.

Overloading the Insertion Operator

Earlier, you learned that you can use the insertion operator with the predefined `ostream` objects `cout` and `cerr` to output the built-in data types because the insertion operator has been overloaded in the `ostream` class. Example 6-13 shows the overloaded `operator<<()` function that provides for output of an int.

Example 6-13 ▶

```
ostream& operator<<(ostream& out, int n);
```

Notice that the `operator<<()` function in Example 6-13 returns a reference to `ostream` and expects two arguments. The first argument is a reference to `ostream` that contains the address of the stream to use for output. The second argument consists of the value to display. The `operator<<()` function returns a reference to `ostream` that enables output chaining. For example, the C++ statement `cout << 2 << 6;` invokes the `operator<<()` function twice. Each time the function is invoked, it returns the address of `cout`, which lets you use `cout` with subsequent values in the statement.

In Chapter 2, you wrote the `print()` method shown in Example 6-14 for the `Video` class.

Example 6-14 ▶

```
void Video::print()
{
  cout << name << ' ' << producer
       << ' ' << quantity << endl;
}
```

As shown in Example 6-14, the `print()` method contains a single `cout` statement that prints the values of the private data members of a `Video` class object. Working with `Video` objects would be easier if you could perform output as follows by using the insertion operator:

```
cout << video_object;
```

To use the insertion operator with an object, you must write an overloaded `operator<<()` function. Example 6-15 shows the declaration for such a function.

Example 6-15 ▶

```
friend ostream& operator<<(ostream& out, const Video& vid_in);
```

The `operator<<()` function must be a friend function in the `Video` class because it is passed an object instead of being invoked by an object. The `operator<<()` function expects two arguments: a reference to an `ostream` object, and a constant reference to a `Video` object. This function returns a reference to an `ostream` object, which enables the use of output chaining. The output displayed by the function can have any format you choose. Example 6-16 shows one possible implementation of the `operator<<()` function for the `Video` class; this implementation prints data members left-justified in a specified field width on separate lines.

Example 6-16 ▶

```cpp
ostream& operator<<(ostream& out, const Video& vid_in)
{
  out << setiosflags(ios::left) << setw(25)
      << "Video Name: " << setw(15) << vid_in.name << endl;
  out << setiosflags(ios::left) << setw(25)
      << "Producer: " << setw(15) << vid_in.producer << endl;
  out << setiosflags(ios::left) << setw(25)
      << "Quantity on Hand: " << setw(15) << vid_in.quantity
      << endl;
  return out;
}
```

Example 6-17 shows a C++ program that instantiates several `Video` objects and then uses the overloaded insertion operator to display the object's data members. To run this program, you must compile two files—Ex6-17.cpp and video.cpp—to generate a single executable file.

Example 6-17 ▶

```cpp
// Ex6-17.cpp
#include "video.h"
int main()
{
  Video rent_one("Titanic", "Cameron Co.", 56);
  Video rent_two("As Good As It Gets", "Jack's Inc.", 35);
  // Use the overloaded insertion operator
  cout << rent_one;
  cout << rent_two;
  return 0;
}
```

Output:

```
Video Name:            Titanic
Producer:              Cameron Co.
Quantity on Hand:      56
Video Name:            As Good As It Gets
Producer:              Jack's Inc.
Quantity on Hand:      35
```

Overloading the Extraction Operator

Overloading the extraction operator (>>) provides an easier way to perform input operations with objects. For example, the `Video` class contains three data members: `name`, `producer`, and `quantity`. You could overload the extraction operator for the `Video` class to get input values for the data members and possibly to test for valid input. Example 6-18 shows the overloaded extraction operator function for the `Video` class. Remember that `operator>>` must be a friend of the `Video` class.

Example 6-18 ▶

```cpp
const int SIZE = 40;
istream& operator>>(istream& in, Video& vid_in)
{
  char temp[SIZE];
  cout << "Enter the video's title: ";
  in.getline(temp, SIZE);
  delete [] vid_in.name;
  vid_in.name = new char[strlen(temp) + 1];
  strcpy(vid_in.name, temp);

  cout << "Enter the producer's name: ";
  in.getline(temp, SIZE);
  delete [] vid_in.producer;
  vid_in.producer = new char[strlen(temp) + 1];
  strcpy(vid_in.producer, temp);

  cout << "Enter the quantity on hand: ";
  in >> vid_in.quantity;
  in.ignore(256,'\n');        // Flush newline
  if(vid_in.quantity < 0)  // Check for valid input
  {
    cout << "Invalid quantity." << endl;
    vid_in.quantity = 0;
  }
  return in;
}
```

Example 6-19 shows a C++ program that uses the overloaded extraction operator with Video objects. To run this program, you must compile two files—Ex6-19.cpp and video.cpp—to create a single executable file.

Example 6-19 ▶

```cpp
// Ex6-19.cpp
#include "video.h"
int main()
{
  Video rent_one;
  Video rent_two;
  // Use the overloaded extraction operator
  cin >> rent_one;
  cin >> rent_two;
  // Use the overloaded insertion operator
  cout << rent_one;
  cout << rent_two;
  return 0;
}
```

The input to and output from this program are as follows:

```
Enter the video's title: The Waterboy
Enter the producer's name: Sandler, Ltd.
Enter the quantity on hand: 35
Enter the video's title: Enemy of the State
```

```
Enter the producer's name: Hackman, Inc.
Enter the quantity on hand: 45
Video Name:            The Waterboy
Producer:              Sandler, Ltd.
Quantity on Hand:      35
Video Name:            Enemy of the State
Producer:              Hackman, Inc.
Quantity on Hand:      45
```

Exercise 6.13 ▶

In Exercise 6.7, you modified the `Time` class. In this exercise, you will modify this class again to overload the insertion (`<<`) and extraction (`>>`) operators. Test your modified `Time` class by running the C++ program saved as Ch6-13.cpp in the Chapter6 folder on your Student Disk. The `Time` class files, time.h and time.cpp, are saved in the Chapter6 folder. Save your modified `Time` class files as timeb.h and timeb.cpp in the Chapter6 folder.

Exercise 6.14 ▶

The C++ program saved as Ch6-14.cpp in the Chapter6 folder on your Student Disk uses the `Student` class. Although you have overloaded the insertion (`<<`) and extraction (`>>`) operators for the `Student` class, the program does not compile. As a result, you do not know whether the operators work correctly. Study the `Student` class files saved as student.h and student.cpp in the Chapter6 folder, and then find and correct the errors so that your Ch6-14.cpp program runs correctly. Do not change the Ch6-14.cpp program. Save your corrected class files as studenta.h and studenta.ccp in the Chapter6 folder.

Exercise 6.15 ▶

Jacob Moretti, the head zookeeper at the Midtown Zoo, has asked you to write a C++ program that reads in data about zoo animals and then prints a list of the animals currently housed at the zoo. Enter the following data from the keyboard:

Animal's Name	Animal's Age	Animal's Weight
Simba Lion	4	300
Geoffrey Giraffe	12	600
Reginald Rhinoceros	3	1200
Willy Wolf	30	80
Darla Dolphin	2	400
Zelda Zebra	15	300
Maynard Monkey	1	20
Alex Ape	5	900
Tony Tiger	30	200
Bertha Bear	10	500

Create an `Animal` class for this program. Overload the insertion (`<<`) and extraction (`>>`) operators for the `Animal` class. Save the completed program as Ch6-15a.cpp and your class files as animal.h and animal.cpp in the Chapter6 folder.

S U M M A R Y

- A stream is a sequence of bytes. The stream classes in C++ provide simpler ways to perform input and output operations.
- The `ios` class is the base class of the stream class hierarchy. Formatting flags are members of the `ios` class that allow you to specify formats for input and output. The `ios` class also contains methods that allow you to specify formats for output.
- A manipulator is a format function that makes formatting easier. You can use manipulators to turn on many formatting flags. C++ offers two types of manipulators: those that expect no arguments and those that expect arguments. You must `#include <iomanip.h>` to use the manipulators that expect arguments.
- Stream error status bits are members of the `ios` class. You use them to represent errors that might occur with an input or output stream.
- The `istream` class is derived from the `ios` class and therefore inherits the data members and methods of the `ios` class. The `istream` class adds the ability to perform input operations and overloads the extraction (`>>`) operator. It also includes methods that provide for the input of data in different ways.
- The `ostream` class is derived from the `ios` class and therefore inherits the data members and methods of the `ios` class. The `ostream` class adds the ability to perform output operations and overloads the insertion (`<<`) operator. It also includes methods that provide for the output of data in different ways.
- The `fstream` class is ultimately derived from the `ios` class and provides for input from and output to data files.
- To perform file input and output in C++, you must `#include <fstream.h>`.
- The `open()` method opens a file, and the `close()` method closes a file. You can use an argument with the `open()` method to specify a file mode.
- The `write()` method writes objects to a file, and the `read()` method populates an object with data read from a file.
- To use the insertion operator (`<<`) with an object, you must overload the insertion operator by writing an `operator<<()` function for the class.
- To use the extraction operator (`>>`) with an object, you must overload the extraction operator by writing an `operator>>()` function for the class.

P R O G R E S S I V E   P R O J E C T S

1. Green Grocery Online Shopping Program

In Chapter 5, you changed the private data members to protected data members in all of the classes you are using for Green Grocery's online shopping program, and then you changed any methods that were impacted by this change. You also derived five new classes from the `GroceryItem` class and used an array of base class pointers to represent a customer's `GroceryItem` list.

In this chapter, you will not use the completed project from Chapter 5—instead, you will use the completed project from Chapter 4 to do the following: use the Stream Input/Output library to format your output in an attractive manner, overload the extraction (`>>`) operator for the `Inventory` and `Customer` classes, and overload the insertion (`<<`) operator for the `Inventory` class. Your main program should read the inventory file simply by using the extraction operator as follows: `fin >> inventory_object_name`. You should get a customer's name and address as follows: `cin >> customer_object_name`. In addition, you should print the names and prices of all `GroceryItem` objects in the `Inventory` object to the screen by using a statement such as `cout << inventory_object_name`.

Save your program as Ch6-pp1.cpp in the Chapter6 folder on your Student Disk, and assign appropriate names to the .h and .cpp files for your classes.

2. Modified Five-Card Stud Poker

In Chapter 5, you added data members and methods to the Player class that allowed you to determine a player's hand and to calculate the winning hand from among the four poker players.

In this chapter, you will use the completed project from Chapter 5 to do the following: use the Stream Input/Output library to format your output in an attractive manner, overload the extraction (>>) operator for the Dealer class, and overload the insertion (<<) operator for the Player class. Your main program should read the card.dat file and get the dealer's name from the keyboard by using the extraction operator as follows: fin >> card_object_name or cin >> dealer_object_name. You should display a player's poker hand as follows: cout << player_object_name.

Save your program as Ch6-pp2.cpp in the Chapter6 folder on your Student Disk, and assign appropriate names to the .h and .cpp files for your classes.

INDEPENDENT PROJECTS

1. WXYZ Radio Station

Maria Chen, the station manager at the WXYZ radio station, has asked you to write a C++ program to manage special broadcasts. Every Saturday evening, WXYZ broadcasts an hour-long radio show that spotlights one recording artist. The file named songs.dat in the Chapter6 folder on your Student Disk contains the title and length for each song. The file named commercial.dat contains a list of commercials and their lengths. During the hour-long broadcast, WXYZ plays a song and then plays a commercial. Your program should read in the data from the two files, then print a program schedule that contains the name of the song to play first, the commercial to play after the first song, the song to play second, the commercial to play after the second song, and so on. The songs and the commercials are stored in the files in priority order. In this project, you must create a Song class and a Commercial class. Use the Stream Input/Output library to format your output in an attractive manner. You should also overload the insertion (<<) and extraction (>>) operators for your classes.

Save your program as Ch6-ip1.cpp in the Chapter6 folder on your Student Disk, and assign appropriate names to the .h and .cpp files for your classes.

2. Label Creation

Raj Singh, the owner of the PrintQuick Company, has asked you to write a C++ program that prints mailing labels for his company. The address data are stored in a file named address.dat in the Chapter6 folder on your Student Disk in the following format:

Name
Street Address
City
State
Zip Code

Your program should print the labels three across and six down the page, with three blank lines appearing between each row of labels, as follows:

Dan Johnson	Fred Murphy	Lynne Swiatek
111 First St.	222 Second St.	333 Third St.
Marengo, IL 60132	Naperville, IL 60512	Woodridge, IL 60517
Jane Li	Ron Zorski	Lou Demma
444 Fourth St.	555 Fifth St.	666 Sixth St.
Downers Grove, IL 60515	Batavia, IL 60432	Wheaton, IL 60544

In this project, you must create an Address class. Use the Stream Input/Output library to format your output in an attractive manner. You also should overload the insertion (<<) and extraction (>>) operators for the Address class.

Save your program as Ch6-ip2.cpp in the Chapter6 folder on your Student Disk, and assign appropriate names to the .h and .cpp files for your classes.

Function Templates and Class Templates

Introduction ▶ In this chapter, you will learn how to create a function template and use parameterized functions in a C++ program. You also will create a class template to describe how the compiler should create new classes automatically, and then you will use the parameterized class templates in C++ programs. Finally, you will see how to use inheritance and templates to derive new classes based on class templates.

Why Use Function Templates?

In Chapter 2, you learned about overloaded functions. To overload a function, you write multiple functions that have the same name. Each overloaded function then acts upon arguments (parameters) of different data types or expects a different number of arguments. When you develop the function definitions for the overloaded functions, you will often find that you write the same code for each function, changing only the data type of the arguments it expects. Example 7-1 shows the function definitions for the overloaded function named `average()` and a C++ program that uses the overloaded functions.

Example 7-1 ▶

```cpp
// Ex7-1.cpp
#include <iostream.h>
// Function declarations
long average(long, long);
double average(double, double);
int main()
{
  long long_value1 = 10, long_value2 = 20;
  double dbl_value1 = 22.7, dbl_value2 = 55.5;
  double dbl_avg;
  long long_avg;
  // Invoke overloaded function
  dbl_avg = average(dbl_value1, dbl_value2);
  cout << "The double average is " << dbl_avg << endl;
  // Invoke overloaded function
  long_avg = average(long_value1, long_value2);
  cout << "The long average is " << long_avg << endl;
  return  0;
}
long average(long num1, long num2)
{
  long avg;
  avg = (num1 + num2) / 2;
  return avg;
}
double average(double num1, double num2)
{
  double avg;
  avg = (num1 + num2) / 2;
  return avg;
}
```

Output:

```
The double average is 39.1
The long average is 15
```

Although overloaded functions are useful, it would be easier if you could write one description or template for the `average()` function and let the C++ compiler use this template to create the functions you need. You would, therefore, write the function only once. Writing a function template saves time because it eliminates some steps.

Function Templates

A **function template** is a description or blueprint for a function. The C++ compiler generates functions based on the data types of the arguments that are passed to those functions. As stated earlier, using function templates allows you to write the template only once; the compiler actually creates multiple functions based on your template. The functions generated by the compiler will differ only in the data types of the arguments they receive.

Writing a Function Template

Example 7-2 shows a function template for the function `average()`. This function is the same one that was shown as an overloaded function in Example 7-1.

Example 7-2 ▶

```
// avg_template.cpp
template <class T> T average(T num1, T num2)
{
  T avg;
  avg = (num1 + num2) / 2;
  return avg;
}
```

As shown in Example 7-2, the keyword `template` is used to tell the compiler that the following C++ statements belong to a template. The `<class T>` that follows the `template` keyword is a symbol that represents a data type. This data type can be used as the return type of the function, the data type of the function's arguments, or the data type of local variables within the function. In Example 7-2, the symbol `T` represents the return data type of the `average()` function template. The two arguments passed to the `average()` function also will have the data type `T`, and the local variable named `avg` is declared to be of data type `T`.

Now, if you use the function template for `average()` and substitute the data type `short` for the data type `T`, your function definition looks like the one shown in Example 7-3.

Example 7-3 ▶

```
short average(short value1, short value2)
{
  short avg;
  avg = (value1 + value2) / 2;
  return avg;
}
```

The C++ compiler generates the code shown in Example 7-3 automatically. If you need a function to find the average of two doubles, the compiler would generate another function based on the same `average()` function template.

Using Function Templates in a C++ Program

Now you can use the function template `average()` in a C++ program. You can include the function template at the beginning of your C++ program or you can `#include` the file that contains the function template.

If you provide a function prototype in the program, the compiler will use this prototype and the template to generate the code for the function. If you don't supply a prototype, the compiler will determine which function to create based on the data type used in the program.

Example 7-4 shows a C++ program that uses the parameterized function named `average()`. A **parameterized function** is a function created from a template in which the specified data type replaces the symbol you used when you wrote the template.

Example 7-4 ▶

```cpp
// Ex7-4.cpp
#include "avg_template.cpp"  // File containing the template
#include <iostream.h>
int main()
{
  long long_value1 = 10, long_value2 = 20;
  double double_value1 = 25.5, double_value2 = 43.7;
  long long_avg;
  double double_avg;
  // Invoke parameterized function; compiler generates code
  long_avg = average(long_value1, long_value2);
  cout << "The long average is " << long_avg << endl;
  // Invoke parameterized function; compiler generates code
  double_avg = average(double_value1, double_value2);
  cout << "The double average is " << double_avg << endl;
  return 0;
}
```

Output:

```
The long average is 15
The double average is 34.6
```

Function Templates with Multiple Data Types

In many cases, you will need to write functions that expect arguments having different data types. You can write function templates for these types of functions by using more than one symbol in the function template. For example, you could expand the `average()` function to find the average of more than two values. You could pass an array of values to the function as well as the number of valid items stored in the array. If the array contains doubles, you must pass in an argument of type double and an argument of type short. The function would return a double, which is the average of the doubles stored in the array.

Example 7-5 shows the function template for the `average()` function revised in this way.

Example 7-5 ▶

```cpp
// avg_temp_rev.cpp
template <class T1, class T2> T1 average(T1 val_array[],
                                         T2 num_values)
{
  T1 avg;
  T1 total = 0;
  int k;
```

```
    for(k = 0; k < num_values; k++)
      total += val_array[k];
    avg = total / num_values;
    return avg;
}
```

In the function template shown in Example 7-5, the function expects two arguments. The first argument's data type is represented by the symbol T1, and the second argument's data type is represented by the symbol T2. The function will return a value of type T1.

Now, the compiler will use this template to generate functions automatically. Example 7-6 shows a C++ program that uses the revised template.

Example 7-6 ▶

```
// Ex7-6.cpp
#include "avg_temp_rev.cpp"  // Contains the revised template
#include <iostream.h>
int main()
{
    long long_vals[] = {568, 3267, 2222, 7890, 2134};
    double double_vals[] = {34.5, 56.7, 67.8, 22.3, 12.2, 67.8};
    long long_avg;
    double double_avg;
    // Invoke the parameterized function; compiler generates code
    long_avg = average(long_vals, 5);
    cout << "The long average is " << long_avg << endl;
    // Invoke the parameterized function; compiler generates code
    double_avg = average(double_vals, 6);
    cout << "The double average is " << double_avg << endl;
    return 0;
}
```

Output:

```
The long average is 3216
The double average is 43.55
```

Exercise 7.1 ▶

The C++ program saved as Ch7-1.cpp in the Chapter7 folder on your Student Disk uses an overloaded print() function. Modify this program to use a function template for print() rather than writing multiple overloaded functions. Save your modified program as Ch7-1a.cpp and your template file as print.cpp in the Chapter7 folder.

Exercise 7.2 ▶

The C++ program saved as Ch7-2.cpp in the Chapter7 folder on your Student Disk finds the largest and second-largest values stored in an array. You have written a function template to perform the processing so that you can use arrays of different data types. This template is stored in the file named largest_two.cpp in the Chapter6 folder. Because the program does not compile, you do not know whether it produces the correct output. Find and fix the syntax errors, and then run the program until it generates the correct output. Save the corrected program as Ch7-2a.cpp and the corrected template file as largest_twoa.cpp in the Chapter7 folder.

Exercise 7.3 ▶

Write a C++ program that calls two functions, each named `divide_by()`. The `divide_by()` functions should divide the first argument passed to them by the second argument passed to them. Both functions should return the result of the division. One `divide_by()` function should accept two integers; the other should accept two doubles. Write a function template for the `divide_by()` function. Save your program as Ch7-3a.cpp in the Chapter7 folder on your Student Disk. Save the template as divide_by.cpp in the Chapter7 folder.

Class Templates

In the previous sections, you wrote a function template to allow the compiler to generate overloaded `average()` functions that performed the same processing but expected arguments of different data types. You also can create class templates in C++. A **class template** provides the compiler with the description or blueprint for an entire class, including its data members and methods. The compiler can then use this description to generate new classes complete with data members and methods.

Like a function template, a class template includes symbols to represent data types. These symbols can represent the data type of a data member, the return type of a method, or the data type of arguments passed to methods.

Writing a Class Template

Many C++ programs will require you to store values in an array, search for values in the array, add values to the array, and delete values from the array. Sometimes you need to store integer values; other times you need to store double values or single characters in the array. Each time you use an array for this purpose, you must write a new class with the same methods and data members. The only difference in these classes involves the data type of the values you store in the array. Ideally, you should be able to write a generic `ArrayList` class and let C++ generate new classes for you based on the data type of the values stored in the array.

To write a class template, you begin by writing the class template definition, then create the class definition using the data type symbols instead of actual data types. The `ArrayList` template shown in Example 7-7 describes a generic class.

Example 7-7 ▶

```
// array_list.h
#ifndef ARRAY_LIST_H
#define ARRAY_LIST_H
const int SIZE = 50;
template <class T> class ArrayList
{
  public:
    ArrayList();  // Constructor
    // Returns 1 if found, 0 if not found
    int find(T value);
    void add(T value);
    int remove(T value);
  private:
    T list_items[SIZE];
    int num_items;
};
#endif
```

To write the class template, you write the keyword `template`; then, within the angle brackets (< >), you write the keyword `class` followed by the symbol(s) that represent data types. After the angle brackets, you write the keyword `class` again followed by the name of the class template.

In Example 7-7, the generic class `ArrayList` contains a constructor and other methods, as well as two data members. The `find()` method expects one argument of type `T`, which represents the value you would like to find in the array. The `find()` method returns an int value of 1 if the value is found and 0 if it does not appear in the array. The `add()` method expects one argument of type `T`, which is the value that will be added to the array. The `remove()` method also expects one argument of type `T`, which is the value to delete from the array. The `remove()` method returns 1 if the value was deleted and 0 if it was not found in the array.

The two data members shown in Example 7-7 are `list_items` and `num_items`. The `list_items` data member is an array of 50 type `T` values, and `num_items` contains the number of values stored in the array.

After writing the class template, you must write the methods and use the symbol(s) you defined in the class template wherever the compiler should substitute an actual data type. Example 7-8 shows the definitions for the `ArrayList` template methods.

Example 7-8 ▶

```cpp
// array_list.cpp
#include "array_list.h"
// Constructor
template <class T> ArrayList<T>::ArrayList()
{
  int k;
  for(k = 0; k < SIZE; k++)
    list_items[k] = 0;  // 0 value
  num_items = 0;
}
template <class T> int ArrayList<T>::find(T value)
{
  int k;
  for(k = 0; k < num_items; k++)
    if(value == list_items[k])
      return 1; // Item found in the array
  return 0;     // Item not found in the array
}
template <class T> void ArrayList<T>::add(T value)
{
  list_items[num_items] = value;
  num_items++;
}
template <class T> int ArrayList<T>::remove(T value)
{
  int j, k;
  for(k = 0; k < num_items; k++)
    if(list_items[k] == value)
    {
      for(j = k; j < num_items - 1; j++)
        list_items[j] = list_items[j + 1]; // Move values
      // Subtract one from the number of items in the array
      num_items--;
      return 1;  // Value deleted
```

```
          }
          return 0;  // Value is not in the array
        }
```

Now that you have written the class template and methods for the `ArrayList` class template, you can create `ArrayList` objects in a C++ program. The C++ program shown in Example 7-9 creates two objects of type `ArrayList`: one maintains a list of integers and the other maintains a list of characters.

Example 7-9 ▶

```cpp
// Ex7-9.cpp
// array_list.cpp contains ArrayList methods
#include "array_list.cpp"
#include <iostream.h>
int main()
{
  // Create an ArrayList object to store integers
  ArrayList<int> int_list;
  // Create an ArrayList object to store characters
  ArrayList<char> char_list;
  // Use ArrayList methods
  int_list.add(10);
  int_list.add(15);
  int_list.add(20);
  if(int_list.find(10))
    cout << "Value found." << endl;
  else
    cout << "Value not found." << endl;
  if(int_list.remove(10))
    cout << "Value deleted." << endl;
  else
    cout << "Value not deleted." << endl;
  char_list.add('a');
  char_list.add('b');
  char_list.add('c');
  if(char_list.find('z'))
    cout << "Value found." << endl;
  else
    cout << "Value not found." << endl;
  if(char_list.remove('a'))
    cout << "Value deleted." << endl;
  else
    cout << "Value not deleted." << endl;
  return 0;
}
```

Output:

```
Value found.
Value deleted.
Value not found.
Value deleted.
```

In the program shown in Example 7-9, the C++ compiler will automatically generate two new classes based on the generic template class `ArrayList`.

Exercise 7.4 ▶

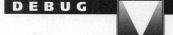

In this exercise, you will use the `ArrayList` class template saved as array_list.h, the `ArrayList` methods saved as array_list.cpp, and the C++ program saved as Ch7-4.cpp in the Chapter7 folder on your Student Disk. Modify the `ArrayList` class template to store an ordered list (that is, a list of values in numeric order). When you add an item to the list, insert it in the proper location in the array. Save your modified files as Ch7-4a.cpp and array_lista.cpp in the Chapter7 folder.

Exercise 7.5 ▶

You have been modifying the `ArrayList` class template to print a particular item stored in the array by passing an integer as an argument to the `print_one()` method. The integer argument indicates the item's position in the array. For example, if you invoke the `print_one()` method and pass the argument 5 to it, the `print_one()` method should print the fifth item in the array—not the item stored in `array[5]`, which is the sixth item. You added a method named `print_one()` to the `ArrayList` class template and a method named `length()` that returns the current length of the list. You also wrote a C++ program to test your new methods. The modified `ArrayList` class template is stored in a file named newlist.h, and the methods for the `ArrayList` class template are stored in a file named newlist.cpp. Your program is saved as Ch7-5.cpp in the Chapter7 folder on your Student Disk. Because the program does not compile, you do not know whether it works correctly. Find and fix the syntax errors, and then run the program. If it does not produce the correct output, find and correct the logic errors. When you have finished, save your debugged program as Ch7-5a.cpp and the corrected template files as newlista.h and newlista.cpp in the Chapter7 folder.

Exercise 7.6 ▶

DEVELOP

Write a class template for a `Set` class. A set is an unordered list of items containing no duplicate values. The `Set` class template should include the following methods:

■ `add()`: Adds an item to the set
■ `find()`: Finds an item in the set and returns its ordinal position (1 for first position, 2 for second position, and so on) in the set of values, or returns –1 if the item does not appear in the set
■ `length()`: Returns the number of items in the set

The `Set` class template should contain the following data members: an array in which to store the items and an integer to keep track of the number of items in the set.

Write a C++ program in which you create two `Set` objects: one to store integer items and another to store doubles. Save your completed program as Ch7-6.cpp, your class template definition as set.h, and your `Set` methods as set.cpp in the Chapter7 folder on your Student Disk.

Container Classes

A **container class** is designed to hold a collection of objects. Container classes usually include methods that allow you to perform the following actions on the collection: insert an object, delete an object, search for an item, sort the objects, and test whether an object is a member. Common data structures, such as arrays, linked lists, stacks, and queues, are examples of container classes—in fact, the `ArrayList` class template created in the previous section is a template for a container class. Many C++ compilers include prewritten container classes as part of their class libraries. The **Standard Template Library** (STL) is a C++ library that includes container classes such as list, queue, stack, set, and vector. It also provides commonly used algorithms, such as sort and search algorithms. Most major compiler vendors now include the STL with their compilers. The STL allows you to write C++ programs that use common data structures without having to write and rewrite classes. To use the STL effectively, you must understand the structure and functioning of templates.

If your compiler does not include container classes as part of its class library, you will probably want to create some. In earlier sections, you have seen how to create a class template for a list implemented as an array. You also might want to implement a class template for a linked list.

Singly Linked List

A **linked list** is a data structure that minimizes the amount of data movement needed to insert data into and delete data from an ordered list. Each element in a linked list is called a node. A **node** contains the data to be stored and a pointer to another node in the list.

A **singly linked list** is a linked list in which each node contains data and a pointer. This pointer points to the next node in the list. Another pointer, called the **head pointer**, points to the first node in the list. The pointer stored in the last node of a singly linked list points to NULL and identifies the end of the list. Figure 7-1 shows a singly linked list that contains five nodes arranged in numerical order.

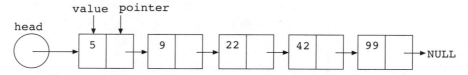

Figure 7-1: Singly linked list

To insert an item in a singly linked list, you modify the pointers, as shown in Figure 7-2.

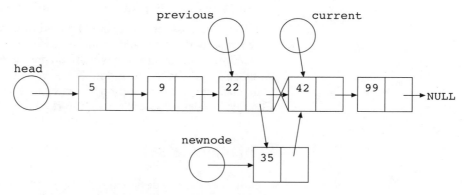

Figure 7-2: Inserting a node into a singly linked list

It doesn't matter which data type is stored in a linked list; the code used for the insertion is the same. The same holds true for the other operations performed on a singly linked list. Container classes usually provide methods that handle inserting, deleting, searching, sorting, and determining whether an item is a member of the collection. When you write a class template for a singly linked list, your class template should provide these methods. By creating a class template for a singly linked list, you provide the description or blueprint for these methods and the data members to be included in the class. The C++ compiler generates new classes for linked lists that contain values of different data types, including user-defined class objects. To take advantage of user-defined objects, you must ensure that the object's class supports the operations defined in the template. For example, if the template requires the assignment of one object to another object, then you must overload the assignment operator. You also must write a template for the nodes in the linked list, which allows you to store different data types in the nodes of a linked list.

The template for a Node shown in Example 7-10 is a template for a structure.

Example 7-10 ▶

```
// node.h
#ifndef NODE_H
#define NODE_H
template <class T> struct Node  // Node is a structure
{
  T value;  // Values of different data types
  Node* next;  // Self-referencing structure
};
#endif
```

Example 7-11 shows the class template and the definition for the methods insert() and print_list() for a singly linked list. (You will develop other methods for this class as an exercise.)

Example 7-11 ▶

```
// linked_list_template.h
#ifndef LINKED_LIST_TEMPLATE_H
#define LINKED_LIST_TEMPLATE_H
#include "node.h"  // Contains Node template

template <class T1> class LinkedList
{
public:
  LinkedList();  // Constructor
  void insert(T1 item);  // Insert in correct location
  void print_list();  // Prints values in the list
protected:
  // Pointer to first Node in the list;
  // it is a pointer to a type T1 Node.
  Node<T1> *head;
};
#endif
```

```cpp
// linked_list_template.cpp
#include <iostream.h>
#include <stdlib.h>
#include "node.h"
#include "linked_list_template.h"
const int TRUE = 1;
const int FALSE = 0;
// Constructor
template <class T1> LinkedList<T1>::LinkedList()
{
  head = NULL;  // Create an empty linked list
}
// Print the list
template <class T1> void LinkedList<T1>:: print_list()
{
  Node<T1>* current; // current is a pointer to a type T1 Node
  current = head;
  while(current != NULL)
  {
    cout << current->value << endl;
    current = current->next;
  }
}
// Add an item to the list in the correct location
template <class T1> void LinkedList<T1>::insert(T1 item)
{
  // current, previous, and newnode are pointers to type T1 Nodes
  Node<T1>* current, *previous, *newnode;
  int found;
  // Allocate memory for a type T1 Node
  newnode = new Node<T1>;
  if(newnode == NULL)
  {
    cout << "Out of heap space." << endl;
    exit(1);
  }

  if(head == NULL)  // List is empty
  {
    newnode->value = item; // Store item in newnode
    // newnode's next pointer should point to NULL
    newnode->next = NULL;
    // head pointer now points to newnode
    head = newnode;
  }
  // Item comes before first node in list
  else if(item < head->value)
  {
    newnode->value = item; // Store item in newnode
    newnode->next =  head;  // newnode points to head
    // head pointer now points to newnode
    head = newnode;
  }
```

```
      else  // General case; find a place for the item
      {
        newnode->value = item; // Store item in newnode
        // previous pointer starts at head of list
        previous = head;
        // current points to second node in list
        current = head->next;
        found = FALSE;
        // Search list for insertion point
        while(current != NULL && found == FALSE)
        {
          // As long as this is true, keep looking for
          // the insertion point.
          if(item > current->value)
          {
            // previous now points to next node
            previous = current;
            // current now points to next node
            current = current->next;
          }
          else
            // When item is less than current's value, then
            // the insertion point is found.
            found = TRUE;
        }
        // Modify pointers to accomplish the insertion
        newnode->next = current;
        previous->next = newnode;
      }
    }
```

Now you can write a C++ program that uses a linked list to maintain a list of short integers, and another linked list that maintains a list of doubles. This program appears in Example 7-12.

Example 7-12 ▶

```
// Ex7-12.cpp
// Contains LinkedList class template
#include "linked_list_template.cpp"
#include <iostream.h>
int main()
{
  LinkedList<short> short_list; // Create new LinkedList class
  LinkedList<double> dbl_list;  // Create new LinkedList class
  // Invoke LinkedList methods
  short_list.insert(22);
  short_list.insert(33);
  short_list.insert(44);
  short_list.print_list();
  dbl_list.insert(22.2);
  dbl_list.insert(33.3);
  dbl_list.insert(44.4);
  dbl_list.print_list();
  return 0;
}
```

Output:

```
22
33
44
22.2
33.3
44.4
```

In the program shown in Example 7-12, the compiler generates two linked list classes automatically: one that contains Nodes that store short integers, and one that contains Nodes that store doubles. The compiler creates these classes as follows:

- When the compiler encounters the statements LinkedList<short> short_list; and LinkedList<double> double_list;, it substitutes <short> or <double> for the T1 symbol in the LinkedList class template.
- In the class template, the compiler creates Node structures for the data type specified (<short> or <double>). It also assigns the data type used for T1 for the T symbol used in the Node template.

Exercise 7.7 ▶

Modify the LinkedList class template to include the remove() method that will delete an item from the LinkedList. The remove() method should accept one argument—the item to be deleted. The LinkedList class template is stored in a file named new_link.h, and the methods are stored in a file named new_link.cpp in the Chapter7 folder on your Student Disk. Use the C++ program saved as Ch7-7.cpp in the Chapter7 folder to test your modifications. Save your modified template files as new_linka.h and new_linka.cpp in the Chapter7 folder.

Exercise 7.8 ▶

You have added a search() method to the LinkedList class that enables you to specify a search item. This method returns 1 if it finds the item and 0 if it does not find the item. You also wrote a C++ program that is saved as Ch7-8.cpp in the Chapter7 folder on your Student Disk to test your new search() method. The program does not generate correct output, however. Find and fix the logic errors in the template files named rev_link.h and rev_link.cpp or Ch7-8.cpp (the test program) in the Chapter7 folder so that the program runs correctly. Save your corrected files as Ch7-8a.cpp, rev_linka.h, and rev_linka.cpp in the Chapter7 folder.

Exercise 7.9 ▶

The command editor for the MegaSwift Operating System uses the # character as the kill character. For example, if a user types the command lisy#t myg#fio#le, then the command editor interprets the input as list myfile. It also interprets the @ character as the line kill character. For example, if a user types the command Listttt myfeiii@, then the command interpreter interprets this input as killing the entire line and the user must begin again. Write a C++ program to simulate this command editor. (*Hint:* A stack would be a good data structure to use for this program.) Create a Stack container class template to use in the program. When you have finished, save your program as Ch7-9a.cpp in the Chapter7 folder on your Student Disk and your template files as stacka.h and stacka.cpp.

Using Inheritance with Class Templates

You can use inheritance with class templates; for example, you can derive a class from the LinkedList class template developed in the previous section. The derived class shown in Example 7-13 resembles the LinkedList class, except the new class will not store duplicate records in the list. The class template and methods for a

NoDups linked list class that uses the LinkedList class template as its base class appear in Example 7-13.

Example 7-13 ▶

```cpp
// no_dups_template.h
#ifndef NO_DUPS_TEMPLATE_H
#define NO_DUPS_TEMPLATE_H
// Contains LinkedList class template
#include "linked_list_template.h"
#include "node.h"
// NoDups class is publicly derived from the LinkedList template
template <class T2> class NoDups : public LinkedList<T2>
{
public:
  NoDups();  // Constructor
  // Overwrite insert to check for duplicates
  void insert(T2 item);
private:  // No new data members
};
#endif

// no_dups_template.cpp
#include "no_dups_template.h"
#include "linked_list_template.h"
// Constructor
template<class T2> NoDups<T2>::NoDups()
{
  // Call base class constructor
  LinkedList<T2>::LinkedList<T2>();
}
// Overwrite insert() inherited from base class
template <class T2> void NoDups<T2>::insert(T2 item)
{
  Node<T2>* current;
  current = head;
  if(head == NULL)  // Empty list
    // Invoke base class insert()
    LinkedList<T2>::insert(item);
  else
  {
    while(current != NULL)
    {
      if(current->value == item) // Check for duplicates
      {
        cout << "Duplicate values not allowed." << endl;
        return;
      }
      else
        current = current->next;
    }
    // Invoke base class insert method
    LinkedList<T2>::insert(item);
  }
}
```

The C++ program shown in Example 7-14 creates a `LinkedList` class object and a `NoDups` class object. The program's output shows that the `NoDups` object does not insert duplicates values in the list.

Example 7-14 ▶

```cpp
// Ex7-14.cpp
#include "linked_list_template.cpp"
#include "no_dups_template.cpp"
#include <iostream.h>
int main()
{
  LinkedList<short> short_list; // Create new LinkedList class
  NoDups<short> no_dup_list;  // Create new NoDups class
  short_list.insert(22);
  short_list.insert(33);
  short_list.insert(44);
  short_list.insert(22); // Inserting a duplicate item is OK
  short_list.print_list();
  no_dup_list.insert(22);
  no_dup_list.insert(33);
  no_dup_list.insert(44);
  no_dup_list.insert(22); // Inserting duplicates not allowed
  no_dup_list.print_list();
  return 0;
}
```

Output:

```
22
22
33
44
Duplicate values not allowed.
22
33
44
```

Exercise 7.10 ▶

The `SmallNums` class was derived from the `LinkedList` class template and is saved as small.h and small.cpp in the Chapter7 folder on your Student Disk. Modify the `SmallNums` class so that it stores only values between 1 and 100 in the list. Save your modified files as smalla.h and smalla.cpp. Use the C++ program saved as Ch7-10.cpp in the Chapter7 folder to test your modifications.

Exercise 7.11 ▶

A class template for a queue is saved as queue.h and queue.cpp in the Chapter7 folder on your Student Disk. You used the `Queue` class for an application you are developing for the Hometown National Bank. You will use a queue to ensure that customers with bad credit backgrounds do not enter the queue for loan processing. Your program, which is saved as Ch7-11.cpp in the Chapter7 folder, does not compile. Find and fix any errors, and then run the program until it produces the correct output. Save your corrected program as Ch7-11a.cpp and the corrected class files as queuea.h and queuea.cpp.

Exercise 7.12 ▶

Derive a new class named `Alpha` by using the `Stack` class template you created in Exercise 7.9 as a base class. The `Alpha` class should allow only alphabetic characters to be pushed on the stack. Write a C++ program to test the `Alpha` class. Save your program as Ch7-12a.cpp and the derived class as alpha.h and alpha.cpp in the Chapter7 folder on your Student Disk.

S U M M A R Y

- Overloaded functions have the same name but accept a different number of arguments or arguments of different data types.
- A function template is a description or blueprint that the compiler uses to generate overloaded functions automatically based on the types of arguments passed to the particular function.
- The keyword `template` tells the compiler that the following C++ code belongs to a template.
- In a function template, `<class T>` defines a symbol that represents a data type. The compiler substitutes an actual data type for this symbol.
- When a C++ program invokes a parameterized function, the compiler automatically generates code for a function based on the template and the data types passed to the function.
- Function templates can include multiple arguments of multiple data types. You must use a unique symbol in the template as a placeholder for each data type.
- A class template provides a description or a blueprint for the compiler to create new classes automatically.
- Like a function template, a class template includes symbols to represent data types. The compiler substitutes actual data types for these symbols when it creates a class.
- To write a class template, you begin by writing the template definition, followed by the class definition (methods) using the symbol(s) from the template definition, instead of actual data types.
- A class template definition begins with the keyword `template`, followed by the keyword `class` and the symbol(s) used in the template to represent data types. The keyword `class` and the symbols appear within angle brackets. After the angle brackets, you use the keyword `class` again, followed by the name of the class template.
- After developing the class template, you write the class methods using the symbol(s) used in the class template wherever the compiler should substitute an actual data type.
- A container class holds a collection of objects. Class templates often are written for container classes. Common data structures, such as arrays, linked lists, stacks, and queues, are examples of container classes.
- You can derive new classes through inheritance using a class template as the base class.

P R O G R E S S I V E   P R O J E C T S

1. Green Grocery Online Shopping Program

In Chapter 6, you used the Stream Input/Output library to format your output in an attractive manner and overloaded the extraction operator (`>>`) for the `Inventory` and `Customer` classes and overloaded the insertion operator (`<<`) for the `Inventory` class.

In this chapter, use the `LinkedList` class template saved as linked.cpp, linked.h, and node.h in the Chapter7 folder on your Student Disk to create a `LinkedList` for your application. Use the `LinkedList` to store the list of `GroceryItem` objects instead of using an array of objects.

Be sure to study the input file named grocery.dat in the Chapter7 folder. An item number has been added for each `GroceryItem` object. Now you must change the implementation of your `GroceryItem` class to include an additional data member and rewrite several methods and constructors.

Also make sure that you have overloaded the operators in the `GroceryItem` class that are used by the `LinkedList` template methods. Change your overloaded comparison operators to do the comparison on the new data member `item_num` instead of the name of each item.

When you are finished, save your program as Ch7-pp1.cpp in the Chapter7 folder on your Student Disk. Assign appropriate names to the .h and .cpp files for your class and class templates.

2. Modified Five-Card Stud Poker

In Chapter 6, you used the Stream Input/Output library to format your output in an attractive manner and overloaded the extraction operator (>>) for the `Dealer` class and overloaded the insertion operator (<<) for the `Player` class.

In this chapter, begin with the project you worked on in Chapter 3 instead of the project from Chapter 6. Modify the program to use a `Stack` class template to create a `Stack` object for the deck of `Card` objects instead of an array of `Card` objects. You may use the `Stack` template saved as stack.h, stack.cpp, and node.h in the Chapter7 folder on your Student Disk. The data file, card.dat, now represents a shuffled deck of cards. Read the data for each `Card` and then push the `Card` on the `Stack`. When a player is dealt a card, the card should be popped from the `Stack`.

Be sure you have overloaded the operators in the `Card` class that are used by the `Stack` template methods.

When you are finished, save your program as Ch7-pp2.cpp in the Chapter7 folder on your Student Disk. Assign appropriate names to the .h and .cpp files for your classes and class templates.

INDEPENDENT PROJECTS

1. Compiler Functionality

One responsibility of the C++ compiler is to ensure that the number of opening and closing curly braces in a program match. Write a C++ program that reads a C++ source code file and determines whether the number of opening and closing curly braces match. (Think of this program as a small part of a compiler.) Use any of your C++ source code files for input and generate meaningful error messages if the numbers of curly braces or parentheses do not match. Use the `Stack` class template saved as stack.h, stack.cpp, and node.h in the Chapter7 folder on your Student Disk to create the `Stack` needed for the implementation of this program. When you have finished, save your program as Ch7-ip1.cpp and your template files as comp_stack.h and comp_stack.cpp in the Chapter7 folder on your Student Disk. Assign appropriate names to the .h and .cpp files for your classes and class templates. You can use any C++ program for your input file.

2. Hospital Room Management

Henry Goodwell, director of the Maybury Municipal Hospital, has asked you to write a C++ program that will help the hospital staff to maintain a list of vacant beds in the hospital rooms. In addition to a room number, your program should keep track of the following information for each hospital room: the number of patient beds, the unit name to which this room is assigned (such as pediatrics, obstetrics, surgery, and so on), and the number of vacant beds in the hospital room. Henry wants a list of the rooms that have vacant beds, ordered numerically by the room number. Write a C++ program using the `LinkedList` class template saved as linked.h, linked.cpp, and node.h in the Chapter7 folder on your Student Disk for this application. The file saved as hospital.dat contains the data for all the hospital rooms in the following format:

room number
unit name
number of beds
number of vacancies

Make sure that hospital staff members can perform the following functions: add a vacancy, delete a vacancy, and list all vacancies. When you have finished, save your program as Ch7-ip2.cpp in the Chapter7 folder on your Student Disk. Assign appropriate names to the .h and .cpp files for your classes and class templates.

C++ Keywords

asm	double	new	switch
auto	else	operator	template
break	enum	private	this
case	extern	protected	throw
catch	float	public	try
char	for	register	typedef
class	friend	return	union
const	goto	short	unsigned
continue	if	signed	virtual
default	inline	sizeof	void
delete	int	static	volatile
do	long	struct	while

Figure A-1: C++ Keywords

ASCII Collating Sequence

APPENDIX B

Symbol	Meaning	ASCII in Decimal Representation	ASCII in Binary Representation	ASCII in Hex Representation
NUL	Null	0	0000 0000	0
SOH	Start of header	1	0000 0001	1
STX	Start of text	2	0000 0010	2
ETX	End of text	3	0000 0011	3
EOT	End of transmission	4	0000 0100	4
ENQ	Enquiry	5	0000 0101	5
ACK	Acknowledge	6	0000 0110	6
BEL	Bell (beep)	7	0000 0111	7
BS	Back space	8	0000 1000	8
HT	Horizontal tab	9	0000 1001	9
LF	Line feed	10	0000 1010	A
VT	Vertical tab	11	0000 1011	B
FF	Form feed	12	0000 1100	C

Figure B-1: Standard ASCII Character Set

Symbol	Meaning	ASCII in Decimal Representation	ASCII in Binary Representation	ASCII in Hex Representation
CR	Carriage return	13	0000 1101	D
SO	Shift out	14	0000 1110	E
SI	Shift in	15	0000 1111	F
DLE	Data link escape	16	0001 0000	10
DC1	Device control one	17	0001 0001	11
DC2	Device control two	18	0001 0010	12
DC3	Device control three	19	0001 0011	13
DC4	Device control four	20	0001 0100	14
NAK	Negative acknowledge	21	0001 0101	15
SYN	Synchronous idle	22	0001 0110	16
ETB	End of transmitted block	23	0001 0111	17
CAN	Cancel	24	0001 1000	18
EM	End of medium	25	0001 1001	19
SUB	Substitute	26	0001 1010	1A
ESC	Escape	27	0001 1011	1B
FS	File separator	28	0001 1100	1C
GS	Group separator	29	0001 1101	1D
RS	Record separator	30	0001 1110	1E
US	Unit separator	31	0001 1111	1F
b/	Space	32	0010 0000	20
!	Exclamation point	33	0010 0001	21
"	Quotation mark	34	0010 0010	22
#	Number sign	35	0010 0011	23
$	Dollar sign	36	0010 0100	24
%	Percent sign	37	0010 0101	25
&	Ampersand	38	0010 0110	26
'	Apostrophe, prime sign	39	0010 0111	27

Figure B-1: Standard ASCII Character Set (continued)

Symbol	Meaning	ASCII in Decimal Representation	ASCII in Binary Representation	ASCII in Hex Representation
(	Opening parenthesis	40	0010 1000	28
)	Closing parenthesis	41	0010 1001	29
*	Asterisk	42	0010 1010	2A
+	Plus sign	43	0010 1011	2B
,	Comma	44	0010 1100	2C
-	Hyphen, Minus sign	45	0010 1101	2D
.	Period, Decimal point	46	0010 1110	2E
/	Forward slash	47	0010 1111	2F
0		48	0011 0000	30
1		49	0011 0001	31
2		50	0011 0010	32
3		51	0011 0011	33
4		52	0011 0100	34
5		53	0011 0101	35
6		54	0011 0110	36
7		55	0011 0111	37
8		56	0011 1000	38
9		57	0011 1001	39
:	Colon	58	0011 1010	3A
;	Semicolon	59	0011 1011	3B
<	Less than sign	60	0011 1100	3C
=	Equal sign	61	0011 1101	3D
>	Greater than sign	62	0011 1110	3E
?	Question mark	63	0011 1111	3F
@	Commercial at sign	64	0100 0000	40
A		65	0100 0001	41
B		66	0100 0010	42
C		67	0100 0011	43
D		68	0100 0100	44
E		69	0100 0101	45
F		70	0100 0110	46
G		71	0100 0111	47
H		72	0100 1000	48

Figure B-1: Standard ASCII Character Set (continued)

Symbol	Meaning	ASCII in Decimal Representation	ASCII in Binary Representation	ASCII in Hex Representation
I		73	0100 1001	49
J		74	0100 1010	4A
K		75	0100 1011	4B
L		76	0100 1100	4C
M		77	0100 1101	4D
N		78	0100 1110	4E
O		79	0100 1111	4F
P		80	0101 0000	50
Q		81	0101 0001	51
R		82	0101 0010	52
S		83	0101 0011	53
T		84	0101 0100	54
U		85	0101 0101	55
V		86	0101 0110	56
W		87	0101 0111	57
X		88	0101 1000	58
Y		89	0101 1001	59
Z		90	0101 1010	5A
[	Opening bracket	91	0101 1011	5B
\	Back slash	92	0101 1100	5C
]	Closing bracket	93	0101 1101	5D
^	Caret	94	0101 1110	5E
_	Underscore	95	0101 1111	5F
`	Grave accent	96	0110 0000	60
a		97	0110 0001	61
b		98	0110 0010	62
c		99	0110 0011	63
d		100	0110 0100	64
e		101	0110 0101	65
f		102	0110 0110	66
g		103	0110 0111	67
h		104	0110 1000	68
i		105	0110 1001	69
j		106	0110 1010	6A
k		107	0110 1011	6B
l		108	0110 1100	6C
m		109	0110 1101	6D
n		110	0110 1110	6E

Figure B-1: Standard ASCII Character Set (continued)

Symbol	Meaning	ASCII in Decimal Representation	ASCII in Binary Representation	ASCII in Hex Representation
o		111	0110 1111	6F
p		112	0111 0000	70
q		113	0111 0001	71
r		114	0111 0010	72
s		115	0111 0011	73
t		116	0111 0100	74
u		117	0111 0101	75
v		118	0111 0110	76
w		119	0111 0111	77
x		120	0111 1000	78
y		121	0111 1001	79
z		122	0111 1010	7A
{	Opening curly brace	123	0111 1011	7B
I	Split vertical bar	124	0111 1100	7C
}	Closing curly brace	125	0111 1101	7D
~	Tilde	126	0111 1110	7E
DEL	Delete	127	0111 1111	7F

Figure B-1: Standard ASCII Character Set (continued)

Index